AF487947

STEAMPRENEURSHIP

STEAMPRENEURSHIP

Through Interdisciplinary Experiential Entrepreneurship

ANTON ANTHONY, ED.S, TH.D.

Anton Anthony, Ed.S, Th.D.

To my wife Shala,

In the quiet moments and the milestones, you have been my unwavering peace and the greatest blessing of my life. This book is dedicated to you, my love, who has faithfully stood by every word and dream.

You promised to always be mine—a listening ear, a shoulder to cry on, and my steadfast supporter in every endeavor. Your vows, "to laugh and cry with me, to protect and trust me, and to give the best of yourself," have been the melody of our life together.

Every step of the way, you've kept that promise, ensuring I never face this world alone. Thank you for being my heart, my cheerleader, and my peace. Here's to continuing our journey, hand in hand, with hearts intertwined.

Forever grateful, forever yours,
Anton

CONTENTS

Technology Integration

Scaling Globally

Innovation in Education: Technologies and Methodologies Influencing Steampreneurship

Step by Step Steampreneurship Implementation

Copyright © 2024 by Anton Anthony, Ed.S, Th.D.

All rights reserved. No part of this book may be reproduced in any manner whatsoever without written permission except in the case of brief quotations embodied in critical articles and reviews.

First Printing, 2024

PREFACE

Author's Journey

My name is Dr. Anton Anthony, and my career in education has been as diverse as it has been fulfilling. Over the years, I have had the privilege of shaping young minds across Georgia—from the most economically disadvantaged districts to affluent communities where education is viewed through the lens of privilege and high expectations. Each role, from a reading specialist to a school principal and now a human resource manager for the third-largest district in Georgia, has offered unique insights and profound experiences that have shaped my vision for a more effective educational system.

Throughout my journey, I have seen firsthand the disparities in educational outcomes driven by socio-economic factors and geographical divides. My experiences have revealed a consistent truth: education, when effectively delivered, has the power to transform lives, regardless of a student's background. This understanding has fueled my determination to redefine and enrich the way we educate our future generations.

With seven books already published, detailing various aspects of educational strategies and leadership, I am turning a new page with a focus on an innovative educational framework that I believe can revolutionize learning on a global scale—Steampreneurship. This framework is not just another educational theory; it is the culmination of years of practical experience and a heartfelt response to the urgent need for a curriculum that resonates with the realities of a globalized world.

PERSONAL REFLECTION

Throughout my years in education across seven different districts in Georgia, I have held many roles: from a reading and 7th-grade English/Language Arts teacher to a principal shaping the direction of entire schools. My journey has granted me a front-row seat to the workings—and failings—of our current educational system. Each role has revealed a consistent, troubling pattern: an overemphasis on standardized testing that measures memory rather than meaning, preparation for tests rather than life.

In one of my roles as a principal, I closely followed the Georgia Department of Education's instructional frameworks for core subjects like ELA, Math, Social Studies, and Science. These frameworks are meticulously designed, not primarily to expand the minds and capabilities of our students, but to prepare them for standardized testing. A test. That's the measure of success. Not whether our students can thrive independently, not whether they possess the skills to be productive citizens, but whether they can fill in the right bubbles on a scantron sheet.

Our school missions often speak of creating students who are "college and career ready," yet this rhetoric fails to confront a critical reality: we are preparing students for a world that is rapidly disappearing. Colleges and our curricula are designed around preparing students for existing jobs—many of which are being automated away by artificial intelligence and other technologies. We're training them for a game where the rules are being rewritten, where entire plays are being erased. As educators, we're at a crossroads. We must ask ourselves if we are merely indoctrinating students to fit into an old mold that is soon to be obsolete.

The reality struck me profoundly one afternoon when I observed a classroom of students preparing for their end-of-year standardized tests. The focus was palpable, the dedication to passing admirable. Yet, it dawned on me: these students could ace this test and still be unprepared for the world they would enter. They were not being equipped with skills to navigate global economics, nor were they taught to innovate or create new pathways in a world where traditional roles no longer apply.

Why are we not preparing students to be the creators of the future? To build the businesses that haven't been dreamed up yet? Our classrooms should be incubators of innovation, where we teach not just mathematics, but how it applies to real-world economic challenges; not just writing, but how persuasive writing forms the backbone of every business proposal and marketing campaign.

VISION OF STEAMPRENEURSHIP THROUGH INTERDISCIPLINARY EXPERIENTIAL ENTREPRENEURSHIP

Vision Statement

The overarching goal of Steampreneurship through Interdisciplinary Experiential Entrepreneurship is to forge a new path in education that integrates global perspectives with hands-on, practical learning experiences. By connecting the dots between interdisciplinary studies and real-world applications, Steampreneurship aims to equip students not just with knowledge, but with the skills and mindset needed to thrive in and contribute to the world.

Steampreneurship is designed to break down the silos of traditional subjects and instead, teach how these disciplines interact and impact our everyday lives through the lens of entrepreneurship. Whether it's understanding the economic impact of imported textiles or exploring the environmental science behind sustainable products, Steampreneurship seeks to make education a relatable, engaging, and deeply relevant process.

As we stand on the brink of launching the AA Steam and Entrepreneurship Academy, my vision is clear: to implement Steampreneurship as our core pedagogical approach. This book aims to outline not only the theoretical foundations and practical applications of Steampreneurship but also to demonstrate its necessity and effectiveness. Through this framework, we can prepare our students to navigate the complexities of the modern world, fostering not just academic success but creating informed, capable, and innovative future leaders.

This is more than just an educational method; it is a movement towards creating a more interconnected and empathetic world through the power of education. Join me in exploring how we can transform our educational systems to not only meet the challenges of today but to anticipate the needs of tomorrow.

THE NEED FOR CHANGE IN GLOBAL EDUCATION

Introduction to Global Education Challenges

The Changing Landscape of Education

As we stand at the intersection of unprecedented technological, economic, and cultural shifts, the landscape of education is being reshaped before our eyes. The 21st-century has ushered in an era where the traditional boundaries of learning are continuously expanded and redefined by digital innovations, global economic interdependence, and a melting pot of cultural interactions.

Technological Advances: The digital revolution has transformed how we access and process information. The rise of the internet, mobile technology, and artificial intelligence has not only introduced new tools for learning but has also changed the very nature of how knowledge is delivered and consumed. According to the World Economic Forum, over 1.2 billion children were out of the classroom globally during the pandemic, catalyzing an unprecedented surge in online learning, with digital platforms seeing a 200-300% increase in usage from previous years (World Economic Forum, 2020). This shift demonstrates not only adaptability but also the potential to permanently alter how education can be accessed.

Economic Shifts: The global economy is increasingly interconnected. The economic events in one part of the world can have ripple effects globally, affecting job markets and industries everywhere. This globalization requires a workforce that is versatile, culturally aware, and equipped with a broad range of skills—from technological proficiency to creative problem-solving. As noted by the OECD in its Future of Education and Skills 2030 project, there is a growing demand for students to be able to tackle complex problems that span multiple disciplines and cultural contexts (OECD, 2018).

Cultural Changes: Our classrooms are more diverse than ever, reflecting broader global migration trends and the movement of people across borders, both physically and virtually. This diversity enriches learning environments but also presents challenges in terms of cultural integration and education equity. UNESCO reports emphasize the importance of incorporating intercultural understanding in the curriculum, highlighting that education systems must evolve to foster respect and inclusion in increasingly multicultural societies (UNESCO, 2019).

These transformative forces compel us to rethink traditional educational paradigms. The static, one-size-fits-all model of yesterday is ill-suited for preparing students for a world where change is the only constant. If we are to equip our students not just to navigate but to thrive in their futures, our approach to education must be as dynamic and adaptable as the world around them. Our students deserve an education that mirrors the complexity of the global stage they will inherit, one that integrates the technological, economic, and cultural dimensions that will define their lives.

Current Educational Challenges

Disconnection from the Global Economy

One of the most critical failings of traditional education systems is their inability to integrate the complex realities of the global economy into everyday learning experiences. This disconnection manifests in curricula that prioritize national history and economy, often at the expense of understanding global economic dynamics and their impacts on local environments. As a result, students graduate with a myopic view of economic forces, ill-prepared for the interdependent world they are entering.

Global Economic Literacy: According to a survey by the National Council on Economic Education, only a minority of students receive any substantial instruction in basic economics, let alone global economic concepts (Walstad, 2019). This lack of economic education is concerning as the world's economies become increasingly interconnected. For instance, a change in the manufacturing industry in China can have ripple effects on job opportunities and product prices in the United States. Yet, our educational frameworks seldom address such global inter-dependencies comprehensively.

Job Market Realities: The modern job market is global, not local. Companies operate across borders, and careers often require interaction with international markets and cultures. A report by the British Council highlighted that employers increasingly value international awareness and experience, as businesses seek to expand their reach across global markets (British Council, 2017). However, traditional education systems rarely offer students the chance to engage with these global perspectives meaningfully.

Technological Disruption: Furthermore, the rapid pace of technological innovation continuously reshapes global industries, creating new job sectors while rendering others obsolete. Research by McKinsey Global Institute predicts that by 2030, up to 375 million workers worldwide will need to switch occupational categories to meet the demands of the shifting global economy (Manyika et al., 2017). Despite this, educational institutions often lag behind, focusing on preparing students for existing jobs rather than developing adaptive skills that could allow them to navigate and excel in a changing economic landscape.

Educational Responses: It's imperative that our education systems evolve to close these gaps. This includes integrating global economic theories and case studies into the curriculum, emphasizing the development of cross-cultural communication skills, and fostering digital literacy that can adapt to new technologies. Only by doing so can we prepare students not just to participate in the global economy but to thrive within it.

The disconnection from the global economy in traditional education limits students' ability to understand and navigate the complex world they are about to enter. By reforming our educational approaches to include more comprehensive global economic education, we can better equip our students for the inevitable challenges and opportunities of the globalized workforce.

Lack of Practical Application

The traditional educational model has long been criticized for its heavy reliance on theoretical knowledge, often at the expense of practical application. This disconnect between what students learn in the classroom and what they apply in real-world settings is not just a disservice to the students; it significantly undermines their ability to function competently in professional environments.

Theoretical vs. Practical Knowledge: A common refrain among educators is the emphasis on "teaching to the test," where the primary focus is on rote memorization and theoretical understanding. While foundational knowledge is essential, the lack of practical, hands-on experiences leaves students ill-prepared for the complexities of real-world problem-solving. A study by the Association for Career and Technical Education (ACTE) highlights that while 81% of students feel that they are being prepared for college, only half believe their education is preparing them for the world of work (ACTE, 2020).

Skills Gap: Employers consistently report a skills gap among graduates, particularly in areas requiring practical abilities such as critical thinking, problem-solving, and interpersonal skills. According to a survey by the National Association of Colleges and Employers (NACE), the ability to apply knowledge in real-world settings is among the top skills employers seek that are not being met by current educational outputs (NACE, 2019). This gap indicates a misalignment between educational objectives and market needs.

Experiential Learning: Experiential learning, which involves learning through doing, could bridge this gap. Educational researchers Kolb and Kolb emphasize that experiential learning not only deepens understanding but also enhances students' abilities to transfer academic concepts to complex situations outside the classroom (Kolb & Kolb, 2005). This method has been shown to improve retention rates, deepen understanding, and better prepare students for professional and personal success.

Integrating Practical Learning: There are various ways to incorporate more experiential learning opportunities within traditional curriculums. These could include project-based learning, where students tackle real-world problems and develop solutions that could be implemented in their communities or businesses. Internships and cooperative education are other avenues where students can gain field-specific skills while still in school, providing them with invaluable insights into their chosen careers.

The educational system's focus on theoretical knowledge while neglecting the practical application has created a generation of students who are often unprepared for the demands of today's job market. By integrating more experiential learning opportunities into our curricula, we can ensure that students not only understand theoretical concepts but can also apply them effectively in their personal and professional lives.

Inequality in Educational Access and Quality

Socio-economic disparities are among the most significant factors influencing educational outcomes. These disparities create unequal access to quality education and resources, resulting in a wide gap in academic achievement between students from affluent backgrounds and those from economically disadvantaged communities. Addressing these inequalities is not only a matter of social justice but also essential for leveraging the full potential of our future workforce.

Impact of Socio-Economic Status on Education: The relationship between socio-economic status (SES) and educational outcomes is well-documented. Research indicates that students from lower SES backgrounds are less likely to have access to high-quality educational resources, including skilled teachers, advanced coursework, and extracurricular opportunities. According to the National Center for Education Statistics, children from low-income families are more than twice as likely to be at risk of poor educational outcomes and drop out before completing high school (NCES, 2020).

Access to Technology and Learning Materials: Socio-economic disparities are also evident in access to technology—a crucial factor in today's learning environment. The digital divide affects students' ability to access online resources, participate in digital learning, and acquire necessary technology skills. A report by Pew Research Center highlights that about one-third of households with children aged 6 to 17 and an annual income below $30,000 a year do not have a high-speed internet connection at home (Pew Research Center, 2018). This lack of access hampers not only the acquisition of digital literacy skills but also students' ability to complete homework and participate in digital learning platforms.

Benefits of an Experientially-Rich Curriculum: An experientially-rich curriculum can help bridge the gap created by socio-economic disparities. Experiential learning opportunities, such as internships, apprenticeships, and project-based learning, provide all students, regardless of background, with hands-on experiences that enhance learning and engagement. These experiences are particularly beneficial for students from disadvantaged backgrounds, as they provide practical skills and real-world insights that traditional classroom settings may not offer.

Case for More Inclusive Education: Integrating experiential learning into the curriculum can make education more inclusive and accessible. It allows students from varied backgrounds to engage with learning in ways that are meaningful, practical, and directly linked to the world outside the classroom. Educational researcher Gloria Ladson-Billings talks about the need for a culturally relevant pedagogy, which uses students' own cultures and backgrounds as vehicles for learning (Ladson-Billings, 1995). This approach helps validate and leverage diverse cultural perspectives, contributing to a richer, more inclusive educational experience.

To combat the effects of socio-economic disparities on educational outcomes, there is a pressing need to design a curriculum that is inclusive and experientially-rich. Such a curriculum not only levels the playing field but also prepares all students to succeed in a diverse and interconnected world.

Globalization and Its Impacts on Education

Economic Globalization

Globalization has profoundly reshaped the world's economies through expanded global trade, the rise of online commerce, and increased international cooperation. These shifts have not only altered how businesses operate but have also had significant implications for education systems worldwide.

Global Trade and Economic Integration: The expansion of global trade has led to a more interconnected world economy, where goods, services, and labor move across borders with greater ease. According to the World Trade Organization, trade has grown 1.5 times faster than global GDP over the last decade, demonstrating the increasing significance of international trade in global economic activity (WTO, 2019). This economic integration demands a workforce that understands international markets, trade regulations, and cultural nuances, underscoring the need for education systems to **incorporate** global economic concepts into their curricula.

Online Commerce and the Digital Economy: The surge in online commerce has created a vast digital economy that transcends national borders. A report by the International Monetary Fund highlights that e-commerce sales have nearly tripled over the past decade, influencing job creation and the skills required in the workforce (IMF, 2020). This shift emphasizes the importance of digital literacy and IT skills in education, preparing students not just for local markets but for a competitive global digital landscape.

International Cooperation and Workforce Mobility: Enhanced international cooperation, facilitated by global organizations and bilateral agreements, has increased workforce mobility and the exchange of knowledge and skills across countries. The Organisation for Economic Co-operation and Development (OECD) notes that international cooperation in education, such as student exchange programs and international research collaborations, is crucial for fostering a globally competent workforce (OECD, 2021). These programs help students gain international exposure and understanding, preparing them for careers that may involve cross-border interactions.

Implications for Education: The implications of these economic changes for education are profound. Curricula need to adapt to prepare students for a globalized job market. This involves not only teaching traditional subjects but also integrating global economic understanding, digital skills, and intercultural competence into everyday learning. Moreover, the ability to navigate an internationalized work environment is becoming increasingly valuable, further stressing the importance of global education initiatives.

Economic globalization challenges traditional educational paradigms and calls for a more globalized curriculum that reflects the realities of the contemporary world. By embracing these changes, educational institutions can better prepare students for the complexities of the global economy.

Cultural Globalization

Cultural globalization refers to the increased interaction and integration of diverse cultures around the world, driven by advances in communication technology, travel, and international commerce. This dynamic exchange of ideas, values, and traditions has profound implications for education, as it both enriches and complicates the learning environment.

Cultural Exchange and Diversity: As people, goods, and media cross borders more freely, students are increasingly exposed to a variety of cultural influences. This exposure can be seen in everything from the multicultural makeup of today's classrooms to the global fusion found in music, food, and entertainment. UNESCO emphasizes the importance of cultural diversity as a source of innovation and creativity, which are crucial for both personal and societal development (UNESCO, 2019). Educators are thus tasked with helping students navigate this complex cultural landscape, promoting understanding and respect for diverse cultural backgrounds.

The Impact of Media and Technology: The global spread of media and technology has played a pivotal role in cultural globalization. According to the Pew Research Center, international broadcast media and social networks have brought global issues and diverse cultures into classrooms and homes, impacting students' perceptions and understanding of the world (Pew Research Center, 2018). This ubiquitous connectivity not only enhances students' awareness of global cultures but also challenges educators to address the varying interpretations and responses to these influences.

Intercultural Competence: With increasing cultural interactions, the ability to effectively communicate and operate across cultures, known as intercultural competence, becomes essential. The American Council on Education highlights that intercultural competence is no longer just an advantageous skill but a necessary one, as workplaces become more diverse and global challenges require cooperative solutions across cultural lines (ACE, 2020). Education systems, therefore, must integrate the development of these skills into their curricula to prepare students for both professional and social environments that are rich in cultural diversity.

Educational Implications: Understanding cultural dynamics is crucial for students not only to thrive in a multicultural world but also to contribute positively to societal development. Curricula need to incorporate comprehensive cultural studies that go beyond traditional Eurocentric perspectives. This includes teaching world histories, languages, and cultures in ways that reflect their interconnectedness and relevance to contemporary global issues.

The role of education in a culturally globalized world is not just to inform but also to transform students into informed global citizens who appreciate cultural diversity and can navigate the complexities it brings with grace and competence.

Technological Advances

The rapid advancement of technology has dramatically transformed the workplace and the nature of social interactions, presenting both challenges and opportunities for the education sector. This transformation has reshaped job roles, demanded new skill sets, and altered the way we communicate, necessitating an educational response that is proactive rather than reactive.

Transformation of the Workplace: Modern workplaces are increasingly driven by digital technologies, from basic computer software to complex artificial intelligence systems. The World Economic Forum's "The Future of Jobs Report" highlights that by 2025, automation and a new division of labor between humans and machines will disrupt 85 million jobs globally, while creating 97 million new roles that are more adapted to the new division of labor (WEF, 2020). This shift underscores the urgency for educational systems to adapt, ensuring students are equipped with relevant skills such as digital literacy, problem-solving in technologically driven contexts, and programming.

Changes in Social Interactions: Technology has also transformed social interactions, particularly among younger generations. Digital platforms like social media have become primary spaces for engaging with peers, sharing information, and learning through informal channels. According to Pew Research

Center, 95% of teens in the United States report they have access to a smartphone, and nearly 45% are online 'almost constantly' (Pew Research Center, 2018). This constant connectivity impacts social skills and the way young people perceive and interact with the world, suggesting that digital citizenship should be an integral part of the curriculum.

Need for Digital Competence: As digital technologies permeate every aspect of personal and professional life, the demand for digital competence in the workforce has escalated. The OECD has emphasized that beyond basic digital literacy, individuals now require a deeper understanding of how to use digital tools responsibly and effectively in a range of contexts (OECD, 2019). Educational systems must thus provide students with robust digital education that includes not only how to use technology but also how to understand its implications on privacy, ethics, and security.

Educational Implications: To keep pace with these changes, education systems need to integrate technology not just as a tool for teaching and learning but as a core subject of study. This involves redesigning curricula to include coding, digital literacy, and cybersecurity, as well as soft skills such as digital communication techniques and online collaboration skills. Moreover, teachers need professional development to become proficient in using and teaching these new tools.

The rapid pace of technological change demands an agile and forward-looking educational system that can prepare students for a future where digital and technological skills are paramount. By aligning education with these technological trends, we can ensure that students are not only capable of navigating a digital world but are also prepared to lead and innovate within it.

The Shortcomings of Traditional Educational Models

Lack of Engagement

One of the most significant shortcomings of traditional educational models is their failure to engage students effectively, particularly as these students prepare to enter a complex, globalized world. Traditional teaching methods often rely heavily on passive learning through lectures and rote memorization, which do not resonate with the needs of today's dynamic and interactive learning environments.

Engagement and Learning Outcomes: Studies have consistently shown that student engagement is crucial for effective learning. A report by Gallup found that engaged students are 2.5 times more likely to say they get excellent grades and are 4.5 times more likely to feel hopeful about their future (Gallup, 2015). However, traditional educational models often fail to foster this engagement, primarily because they do not cater to diverse learning styles or incorporate students' interests and real-world issues into the curriculum.

Impact on Student Interest and Motivation: Traditional classrooms often emphasize compliance and uniformity, which can stifle creativity and discourage critical thinking. This can lead to disinterest and disengagement, particularly among students who do not see the relevance of what they are learning to their lives and future careers. A study by the National Research Council concluded that engaging learning experiences are those that are both personally meaningful and connected to the broader social context, something traditional models frequently overlook (National Research Council, 2012).

Inadequacy in Preparing for Global Challenges: In the context of globalization, traditional educational methods are particularly inadequate. They often lack a global perspective and fail to integrate the skills necessary to navigate a globalized environment, such as cross-cultural communication and global awareness. The Asia Society's Partnership for Global Learning argues that an emphasis on 21st-century skills, including global literacy, is essential for preparing students to participate in the global community and economy (Asia Society, 2018).

Educational Implications: To address these challenges, educational models need to move beyond traditional methods and embrace approaches that enhance engagement through relevance and interactivity. This means adopting more project-based learning, integrating technology in meaningful ways, and making learning contextual and connected to real-world issues.

The traditional focus on passive learning and standardized testing does not adequately prepare students for the complexities of the modern world. To cultivate a more engaged and capable generation, educational systems must evolve to foster active learning environments that encourage curiosity, creativity, and critical thinking.

Standardization vs. Personalization

Traditional educational systems often operate on a "one-size-fits-all" philosophy, standardizing curriculum, teaching methods, and assessment criteria to ensure uniformity across different levels and schools. However, this approach overlooks the individual needs, interests, and abilities of students, stifling potential growth and innovation.

Critique of Standardization

Uniformity Over Flexibility: Standardized education emphasizes uniformity and compliance, which can be detrimental in a rapidly changing global landscape. It assumes all students learn the same way at the same pace, which is contrary to what educational research suggests about individual learning processes. According to the National Center for Biotechnology Information, cognitive research shows significant variability in how students comprehend and process information, indicating that a rigid educational framework is often counterproductive (NCBI, 2017).

Impact on Student Creativity and Motivation: Standardization can demotivate students who might not fit the traditional learning mold or who could excel in less conventional areas not covered by the standard curriculum. A report by the Organization for Economic Co-operation and Development (OECD) highlights that student motivation and performance improve when they feel their learning is tailored to their personal interests and needs (OECD, 2016).

The Case for Personalization

Personalized Learning Environments: Moving towards a personalized, student-centered approach can significantly enhance learning outcomes. Personalized learning acknowledges and adapts to the varied strengths, weaknesses, and interests of individual students. The Bill and Melinda Gates Foundation funded research on personalized learning, finding that schools that implemented personalized learning strategies saw significant gains in student achievement, particularly in reading and math (Gates Foundation, 2014).

Technology as an Enabler: Advances in educational technology have made it easier to implement personalized learning at scale. Adaptive learning technologies, which adjust the difficulty of tasks based on a student's performance, can cater to diverse learning needs and help bridge the gap between different ability levels within a classroom.

Preparing for the Future: Personalized education not only addresses individual learning styles but also prepares students for the future by fostering skills like critical thinking, creativity, and adaptability—qualities that are essential in a globalized, rapidly evolving world. The Center for Curriculum Redesign emphasizes that personalization helps develop the whole person, equipping students with the competencies needed for the 21st century (Center for Curriculum Redesign, 2015).

The shift from a standardized to a personalized learning model is not just beneficial but necessary for cultivating an education system that is inclusive, flexible, and capable of preparing students for the complexities of modern life and work.

Theoretical vs. Experiential Learning

While traditional educational models often prioritize theoretical knowledge, there is a growing recognition of the need to integrate more experiential learning opportunities that mirror the complexities of the real world. Experiential learning emphasizes engaging with and learning from real-life, practical experiences rather than solely from abstract concepts or passive absorption of information.

Limitations of Theoretical Learning

Lack of Context and Application: Theoretical learning can sometimes be disconnected from its practical applications. This disconnection can make it challenging for students to understand the relevance of what they are learning and how to apply it in real-life situations. According to research published in the Journal of Education for Business, students often struggle to transfer theoretical knowledge to practical applications without direct experience (Journal of Education for Business, 2018).

Engagement and Retention Issues: Research has shown that purely theoretical instruction may fail to fully engage students, impacting their ability to retain information. A study by the Association for Psychological Science found that students learn better and retain information longer when they are actively engaged in the learning process through doing rather than observing (Association for Psychological Science, 2019).

Advantages of Experiential Learning

Enhanced Understanding and Retention: Experiential learning allows students to deepen their understanding by applying knowledge in real-world contexts. This approach not only improves retention but also helps develop higher-order thinking skills. According to Kolb's Experiential Learning Theory, the process of doing, reflecting, theorizing, and experimenting leads to more profound learning experiences (Kolb, 1984).

Preparation for Real-World Challenges: Integrating experiential learning prepares students for the complexities of the real world. It equips them with the critical thinking, problem-solving, and interpersonal skills necessary to navigate and succeed in a rapidly changing global environment. A report by the National Service Learning Clearinghouse emphasizes that students who participate in experiential learning are better prepared to meet the demands of the workplace and are more adaptable to new situations (National Service Learning Clearinghouse, 2020).

Cultivation of Soft Skills: Experiential learning also fosters the development of soft skills such as communication, teamwork, and leadership. These skills are increasingly important in diverse and collaborative professional settings. A study by the Business Higher Education Forum highlights the significant demand for soft skills in the workforce, noting that experiential learning through internships and similar opportunities can bridge the gap between academic skills and workplace needs (Business Higher Education Forum, 2017).

The case for integrating more experiential learning opportunities into education is compelling. By doing so, educational institutions can ensure that learning is not only more engaging and relevant but also more effective at preparing students for the professional and personal challenges of the future.

Summing Up the Imperatives

As we have explored throughout this chapter, traditional educational models are increasingly misaligned with the demands of a globalized, technologically advanced, and culturally diverse world. The shortcomings of these models—such as their emphasis on standardization over personalization, theoretical knowledge over practical application, and a general disengagement from real-world complexities—underscore the urgent need for a transformative approach to education.

Key Failures of Traditional Models:

1. **Disconnection from the Global Economy:** Traditional education often fails to incorporate the interconnectedness of today's global economies, leaving students ill-prepared for a workforce that transcends national borders.

2. **Lack of Practical Application:** There is a critical gap between the theoretical knowledge taught in schools and its application in real-world settings, which compromises the readiness of students to tackle real-life challenges effectively.

3. **Standardization vs. Personalization:** The one-size-fits-all approach neglects the diverse needs and potentials of individual learners, stifling creativity and innovation.

4. **Theoretical vs. Experiential Learning:** Traditional methods focus heavily on passive learning, which does not engage students as effectively as experiential learning, nor does it foster essential skills such as critical thinking and problem-solving.

These issues are not just educational but societal, as the quality and relevance of education directly impact economic stability, social cohesion, and individual fulfillment.

Bridge to Steampreneurship Through Interdisciplinary Experiential Entrepreneurship

In response to these pressing challenges, a new educational paradigm is not only beneficial but essential. The introduction of Steamprreneurship through Interdisciplinary Experiential Entrepreneurship in the forthcoming chapters represents a pivotal shift towards an integrated, experiential, and globally-oriented approach to learning. Steamapreneurship aims to bridge the gaps identified in traditional educational practices by focusing on:

Interdisciplinary Learning: Fostering an understanding that combines multiple subject areas, allowing students to solve complex problems with a holistic perspective.

Experiential Learning: Placing students in direct contact with real-world scenarios where they can apply their knowledge and refine their skills in authentic contexts.

Global and Cultural Awareness: Preparing students to operate in a global environment with a keen understanding of and respect for cultural diversity.

Entrepreneurial Thinking: Encouraging innovation, problem-solving, and a proactive approach to creating value in the economy.

The urgency for implementing Steampreneurship comes from a critical need to equip our students not only to succeed in their careers but to excel as capable, responsible members of a global society. As we transition to the detailed exploration of Steampreneurship, consider it not just as an educational strategy but as an essential framework for cultivating the next generation of learners, leaders, and innovators.

~ 2 ~

FOUNDATIONS OF STEAMPRENEURSHIP

Defining Steampreneurship

Detailed Definition

Steampreneurship represents a transformative educational framework designed to meet the demands of the 21st-century learner. It integrates various educational disciplines into a cohesive and engaging learning experience that transcends traditional classroom boundaries. Steampreneurship synthesizes the essential elements of interdisciplinary learning, experiential learning, and entrepreneurship education into a single, robust model that prepares students to navigate and thrive in complex, real-world environments.

Interdisciplinary Learning: At the core of Steampreneurship is the belief that real-world problems are not confined to single subject areas but require a comprehensive understanding across various fields. Steampreneurship thus encourages the integration of subjects such as mathematics, science, social studies, and language arts, allowing students to approach complex problems with a holistic perspective. This approach not only enhances cognitive abilities but also fosters a deeper understanding of how interconnected our world is. The interplay of different disciplines mirrors the complexity of real-world scenarios, preparing students to think critically and creatively.

Experiential Learning: Steampreneurship emphasizes learning through direct experience, where theoretical knowledge meets practical application. This component of Steampreneurship involves hands-on projects, simulations, internships, and community engagement, all designed to provide students with real-life challenges and opportunities to apply what they have learned in meaningful contexts. According to Kolb's theory of experiential learning, effective learning is seen when a person progresses through a cycle of experiencing, reflecting, thinking, and acting, which leads to deeper understanding and skill development (Kolb, 1984).

Entrepreneurship Education: Entrepreneurship within Steampreneurship goes beyond teaching students how to start businesses. It embeds the spirit of innovation and problem-solving across all learning activities. This aspect of Steampreneurship cultivates an entrepreneurial mindset, encouraging students to think like innovators and problem solvers, irrespective of the career paths they choose. This approach aligns with the evolving economic landscape where entrepreneurial skills such as adaptability, risk-taking, and proactive problem-solving are increasingly crucial (Drucker, 1985).

Steampreneurship is not just a pedagogical theory but a practical response to the educational needs of today's students, who must navigate a globalized, technologically advanced, and culturally diverse world. By integrating these components, Steampreneurship offers a dynamic and robust educational experience that prepares students not only academically but also socially and economically for the challenges of the future.

This comprehensive definition of Steampreneurship underpins its role as a critical educational model for contemporary learning environments, reflecting a deep understanding of how interconnectivity, practical experience, and entrepreneurial thinking are vital in shaping capable, resilient, and innovative individuals.

Theoretical Underpinnings

Steampreneurship is deeply rooted in established educational theories that emphasize active, connected, and personalized learning. Two of the most relevant theories supporting the framework of Steampreneurship are constructivism and connectivism. These theories provide a scholarly foundation for why this innovative approach to education is effective and necessary in today's rapidly evolving learning environments.

Constructivism

Constructivism posits that learners construct their own understanding and knowledge of the world, through experiencing things and reflecting on those experiences. When students encounter something new, they have to reconcile it with their previous ideas and experiences, sometimes changing what they believe, or sometimes discarding the new information as irrelevant. In both cases, they are actively constructing their own knowledge. This theory is championed by educational theorists like Jean Piaget and Lev Vygotsky, who argue that learning is a deeply personal process that is mediated by each learner's previous knowledge and experiences (Piaget, 1954; Vygotsky, 1978).

In the context of Steampreneurship, constructivism supports the integration of experiential learning where students are not mere recipients of transmitted knowledge but active participants in creating their path of understanding. This is especially effective in an interdisciplinary setting where students can see how different fields connect and influence each other, thus constructing a more integrated and holistic view of knowledge.

Connectivism

Developed by George Siemens and Stephen Downes, connectivism stresses the importance of networks and connections in the learning process, particularly in the digital age. According to connectivism, the learning process is no longer individual but collective. Knowledge is distributed across a network of connections, and learning consists of the ability to construct and traverse those networks (Siemens, 2005).

Steampreneurship leverages connectivism by emphasizing the importance of digital literacy and collaborative learning environments. It encourages students to use technology to connect with information sources and each other, thus enhancing their learning by accessing and contributing to a shared pool of global knowledge. In a world where knowledge is continuously expanding and evolving, the ability to navigate and grow personal learning networks is invaluable.

Integration of Theories in Steampreneurship

Both constructivism and connectivism inform the pedagogical approach of Steampreneurship by emphasizing learning as an active, contextualized process of building connections between ideas, disciplines, and people. They advocate for educational experiences that mirror real-world interactions and complexities, thereby preparing students for the demands of the modern workplace and society.

These theoretical foundations ensure that Steampreneurship is not just practically relevant but also pedagogically robust, combining the strengths of active, experiential learning with the expansive potential of digital and networked learning environments.

Historical Context

The evolution of educational models leading up to Steampreneurship reflects a progressive shift toward more integrative, engaging, and applicable learning strategies. This historical trajectory has been shaped by various educational innovations and their inherent shortcomings, each contributing to the development of Steampreneurship as a comprehensive response to modern educational demands.

From Traditional to Progressive Education

Traditional Education Models: Historically, education was primarily about rote learning and memorization, with a strong focus on discipline-specific knowledge. This model was largely influenced by industrial-age priorities, which valued conformity and standardization, qualities that were reflected in the classroom (Kliebard, 1995). The teacher-centered approach dominated, where students were passive recipients of information.

Progressive Education Movement: Reacting to the rigidity of traditional methods, the progressive education movement emerged in the early 20th century, championed by thinkers like John Dewey. Dewey criticized traditional education for its lack of relevance to students' lives and advocated for "learning by doing." He emphasized the importance of experience in education and believed that learning should be student-centered and grounded in real-life activities (Dewey, 1938).

Rise of Experiential and Interdisciplinary Learning

Experiential Learning: Building on Dewey's ideas, experiential learning gained prominence, emphasizing engagement, inquiry, and reflection. David Kolb further advanced this concept in the 1980s with his Experiential Learning Theory, which presented a four-stage cycle of learning that underlined the importance of experiencing, reflecting, thinking, and acting as a continuous process (Kolb, 1984).

Interdisciplinary Learning: The latter part of the 20th century saw a growing recognition of the limitations of siloed knowledge. The interdisciplinary approach began to take shape, aiming to synthesize knowledge across multiple disciplines to tackle complex problems holistically. This approach was seen as crucial for developing critical thinking and problem-solving skills applicable to the interconnected modern world (Newell, 1990).

Integration with Entrepreneurship Education

Entrepreneurship Education: As the global economy began to value innovation and entrepreneurship increasingly, educational models began to incorporate these elements. Entrepreneurship education initially focused on business skills but gradually expanded to include fostering an innovative mindset and entrepreneurial spirit across various fields (Vesper and Gartner, 1997).

Development of Steampreneurship: Steampreneurship emerged as a culmination of these educational advancements, integrating the hands-on, reflective nature of experiential learning with the holistic view of interdisciplinary studies, further enriched by entrepreneurship education. Steampreneurship addresses past educational shortcomings by providing a framework that is not only multidimensional but also directly linked to real-world applications and future career skills. (Anthony 2024)

Steampreneurship represents a synthesis of historical educational insights and practices, designed to equip students with the comprehensive skills needed in today's dynamic and interconnected world. It is an embodiment of the shift from passive reception of knowledge to active creation, application, and continuous adaptation.

Core Components of Steampreneurship

Interdisciplinary Approach

The interdisciplinary approach within Steampreneurship aims to dismantle the traditional silos that have long defined and confined educational disciplines. By fostering an educational environment where subjects such as mathematics, science, social studies, and language arts are integrated, Steampreneurship promotes a holistic understanding of complex real-world issues. This section explores how interdisciplinary learning not only enriches educational experiences but also equips students with the comprehensive skills necessary to navigate the complexities of modern life.

Breaking Down Silos

Nature of Complex Problems: Today's global challenges—such as climate change, economic inequality, and technological disruptions—are inherently interdisciplinary. They do not adhere to the neat boundaries of traditional academic disciplines.

Addressing these issues effectively requires a synthesis of knowledge from multiple fields. Steampreneurship leverages this necessity by structuring learning around real-world problems and projects that require students to draw on and integrate multiple disciplines (Jacobs, 1989).

Holistic Learning Experiences: By integrating disciplines, Steampreneurship helps students see connections between different areas of knowledge, promoting deeper understanding. For instance, a project on environmental sustainability might involve science (understanding ecosystems), mathematics (calculating carbon footprints), social studies (exploring policies and their impacts), and language arts (communicating findings and advocating for change). This holistic approach not only enhances academic learning but also encourages students to think critically and creatively about how they can contribute to solving global issues (Boix Mansilla & Duraising, 2007).

Educational Benefits

Enhanced Cognitive Skills: Interdisciplinary learning has been shown to enhance critical thinking, problem-solving, and analytical skills. A study by Boix Mansilla and colleagues at Project Zero at Harvard University demonstrated that students engaged in interdisciplinary work were better at recognizing bias, thinking critically, and applying knowledge creatively in new situations (Boix Mansilla et al., 2009).

Increased Engagement and Motivation: When students understand the relevance of their studies to real-world issues, their motivation and engagement can increase significantly. This engagement is further enhanced by the active learning environment in Steampreneurship, where students are not passive recipients of predetermined knowledge but active participants in constructing their understanding and solutions (Wang et al., 2018).

Challenges and Solutions

Curriculum Design: Designing an interdisciplinary curriculum can be challenging due to the traditionally segmented structure of school curricula. However, Steampreneurship addresses these challenges by promoting flexibility in curriculum design and encouraging educators to develop units and projects that cross disciplinary boundaries. Professional development and collaborative planning among teachers are crucial for effective implementation (Newell, 1990).

Assessment Strategies: Traditional assessment methods often do not capture the depth and breadth of interdisciplinary learning. Steampreneurship advocates for more dynamic assessment strategies that are project-based and reflective of students' critical thinking, collaboration, and innovation skills (Frodeman, 2017).

The interdisciplinary approach in Steampreneurship provides students with a richer, more connected view of knowledge, preparing them to tackle complex problems with a well-rounded perspective. This approach not only enhances academic skills but also fosters a deeper understanding of and engagement with the world.

Experiential Learning in Steampreneurship

Experiential learning, a core component of Steampreneurship is predicated on the idea that the most effective learning occurs when students are actively engaged in experiences that mimic real-world challenges. This section details how Steampreneurship incorporates experiential learning through project-based learning, internships, and field experiences, providing students with tangible, hands-on opportunities to apply classroom knowledge in practical settings.

Project-Based Learning (PBL)

Integration and Application: PBL is a dynamic classroom approach in which students actively explore real-world problems and challenges and acquire a deeper knowledge through active exploration of real-world challenges and problems. In Steampreneurship, PBL involves students in complex tasks, culminating in realistic products, presentations, or performances. It combines knowledge from various disciplines, allowing students to employ skills from science, math, technology, and the arts in integrated ways (Thomas, 2000).

Benefits of PBL: Studies have shown that PBL not only improves student engagement and learning but also boosts retention rates and helps develop higher order cognitive skills. Students engaged in PBL settings perform better in problem-solving and have higher levels of engagement and motivation due to the relevance of the tasks to real-life situations (Bell, 2010).

Internships and Apprenticeships

Real-World Experience: Internships and apprenticeships are critical in Steampreneurship as they provide students with direct exposure to professional environments. These experiences allow students to connect theoretical knowledge with practical applications, bridging the gap between academic learning and professional employment.

Skill Development: Internships foster numerous soft skills, including teamwork, communication, and professional responsibility. Research has indicated that internships significantly enhance the employability of students by providing them with the hands-on skills and experience that employers value (NACE, 2019).

Field Experiences

Learning Outside the Classroom: Field experiences involve activities that take students out of the classroom to learn in a real-world context. These might include field research, community service projects, or participation in cultural events, all of which provide immersive learning opportunities that deepen students' understanding of course content.

Enhanced Learning Outcomes: Field experiences are shown to improve critical thinking and analysis skills by allowing students to engage directly with the material in a contextual setting. These experiences also heighten cultural awareness and sensitivity, particularly when students interact with diverse populations or ecosystems (Kuh, 2008).

Integration with Steampreneurship

Synergistic Learning: In Steampreneurship, these experiential learning components are not standalone experiences but are integrated in a manner that allows each type of learning to inform the others. For instance, insights gained during an internship might spark a project idea that can be executed through PBL, or observations from a field experience might be analyzed and developed further in a classroom setting.

Experiential learning in Steampreneurship represents a shift from traditional education models to a more dynamic, practical approach where learning is active, contextual, and deeply interwoven with real-world applications. It prepares students not just to think critically and solve problems, but to act with insight and creativity in situations they will encounter outside the classroom.

Entrepreneurship Education in Steampreneurship

Entrepreneurship education is designed to instill the essential skills of innovation, creativity, and business acumen. This section explores how entrepreneurship education within

Steampreneurship not only prepares students to start and manage businesses but also cultivates a mindset that is vital for addressing modern economic and societal challenges.

Fostering Creativity and Innovation

Cultivating an Entrepreneurial Mindset: Entrepreneurship education goes beyond the mechanics of business creation and management. It fosters a mindset oriented towards innovation and opportunity recognition. This mindset encourages students to think critically and creatively about solutions to wide-ranging challenges, from local community issues to global problems (Volkmann, 2009).

Enhancing Problem-Solving Skills: Entrepreneurial thinking involves identifying needs and opportunities, generating innovative solutions, and executing these solutions effectively. The process enhances students' problem-solving and decision-making skills, making them more adaptable and capable of navigating complex scenarios (Fayolle, 2015).

Integrating Business Skills

Practical Business Knowledge: Within Steampreneurship, entrepreneurship education provides practical knowledge in finance, marketing, strategic planning, and operations management. This knowledge is crucial not only for business success but also for understanding the broader economic environment in which businesses operate.

Application to Real-World Challenges: Applying business skills to real-world contexts within the educational setting allows students to see firsthand how economic principles impact everyday life and global markets. This applied learning supports deeper engagement and retention of knowledge (Jones & English, 2004).

Educational Outcomes

Economic Understanding and Literacy: Entrepreneurship education enhances students' understanding of economic concepts and their applications, preparing them for more informed participation in the economy as consumers, employees, and leaders (Charney & Libecap, 2000).

Skill Development: Students acquire a range of transferable skills through entrepreneurship education, including leadership, financial literacy, networking, resource management, and ethical decision-making. These skills are broadly applicable and highly valued across various career paths.

Research Support

Studies have shown that students who participate in entrepreneurship education programs are more likely to start their own businesses and are better equipped with the skills necessary to innovate within existing organizations. The exposure to entrepreneurial activities significantly impacts students' entrepreneurial intentions and their subsequent career choices (Lautenschläger & Haase, 2011).

Entrepreneurship education within Steampreneurship is not just about business creation; it is about cultivating a robust set of skills and a mindset that embraces innovation, critical thinking, and problem-solving. These elements are crucial in a rapidly changing world where economic and societal challenges demand novel and effective solutions.

Benefits of Steampreneurship

Steampreneurship offers significant benefits in enhancing student engagement, deepening understanding, and improving knowledge retention. This section explores these benefits, supported by research, to demonstrate how Steampreneurship effectively addresses some of the traditional educational system's key limitations.

Enhanced Student Engagement

Active Learning Strategies: Steampreneurship's foundation in active learning strategies—such as project-based learning, real-world problem-solving, and collaborative tasks—naturally increases student motivation and interest. By engaging students in meaningful activities that have direct applications beyond the classroom, Steampreneurship makes learning more relevant and dynamic. A study by Prince (2004) found that active learning leads to greater student engagement and enthusiasm, which are critical drivers of educational success.

Relevance to Real Life: Steampreneurship connects academic concepts to real-world situations, helping students understand the practical importance of their studies. This relevance is crucial for maintaining student interest and motivation, as noted by Crouch and Mazur (2001), who observed increased student engagement when learning activities were clearly connected to real-life applications.

Deeper Understanding and Retention

Interdisciplinary Learning: By integrating multiple disciplines, Steampreneurship helps students make connections between different areas of knowledge, leading to a more comprehensive understanding of complex concepts. This holistic approach fosters cognitive skills such as critical thinking and problem-solving. Research by Boix Mansilla and Dawes Duraisingh (2007) highlights that students who engage in interdisciplinary studies often achieve higher levels of comprehension and are better able to synthesize and apply knowledge in new contexts.

Experiential Learning: The experiential component of Steampreneurship ensures that students do not just learn theoretical content but also apply it, which significantly enhances knowledge retention. Kolb's Experiential Learning Theory (1984) supports this, suggesting that students learn best through a cyclical process of experiencing, reflecting, thinking, and acting. This theory is echoed by findings from Eyler (2009), who reported that experiential learning environments contribute to improved retention rates and the ability to transfer knowledge to different situations.

Facilitating Knowledge Transfer: The ability to apply learned knowledge to new and varied contexts is a standout benefit of Steampreneurship. This transfer is critical in today's rapidly evolving world, where individuals frequently face novel challenges. Steampreneurship's focus on real-world applicability prepares students to adapt their learning to these challenges effectively. A study by Perkins and Salomon (2012) indicates that students trained in environments that emphasize real-world application are more adept at transferring knowledge to new situations.

The benefits of Steampreneurship—enhanced engagement, deeper understanding, and improved retention—position Steampreneurship as a highly effective educational model. By making learning more relevant, integrative, and applicable, Steampreneurship not only addresses educational needs but also prepares students for professional and personal success in a complex global landscape.

Preparation for Real-World Success

Steampreneurship is meticulously designed to prepare students for the myriad challenges of the modern world. By integrating a diverse set of essential skills into the curriculum—such as critical thinking, collaboration, and adaptability—Steampreneurship ensures that students are not only ready to enter the workforce but are equipped to excel in a globalized society.

Developing Critical Thinking Skills

Analytical and Evaluative Skills: Steampreneurship emphasizes critical thinking by challenging students to analyze and evaluate information from a variety of sources and disciplines. Through interdisciplinary projects, students learn to approach problems from multiple perspectives, enhancing their ability to think deeply and critically. Research by Abrami et al. (2008) supports that teaching methods that promote inquiry and argumentation significantly improve critical thinking skills in students.

Problem-solving in Complex Situations: By engaging in real-world projects and simulations, students in Steampreneurship settings encounter complex, unstructured problems similar to those they will face in their professional lives. This exposure helps develop agile problem-solving skills, an ability highly valued in today's dynamic work environments. Wagner (2010) notes that the ability to tackle complex problems is a key differentiator for individuals in the workforce.

Enhancing Collaboration

Teamwork and Communication: Steampreneurship promotes collaboration by involving students in group projects where they must work together to achieve common goals. This cooperative learning not only improves communication skills but also teaches students how to negotiate and manage conflicts effectively. Johnson and Johnson's meta-analysis (2009) highlights that cooperative learning experiences are associated with higher achievement and more favorable interpersonal relationships.

Cross-cultural Interactions: In our increasingly global society, the ability to collaborate across cultural boundaries is crucial. Steampreneurship fosters this skill through international projects and virtual collaborations with peers from different cultural backgrounds. Research by Olson and Kroeger (2001) shows that students who engage in cross-cultural interactions gain better global awareness and interpersonal skills.

Cultivating Adaptability

Flexibility in Changing Environments: The rapid pace of change in today's world requires individuals to be highly adaptable. Steampreneurship prepares students for this reality by exposing them to varied learning environments and challenges, encouraging a mindset that is flexible and open to change. A study by Pulakos et al. (2000) found that adaptability is a critical factor in performance, especially in complex and changing job environments.

Innovation and Creativity: Adaptability in Steampreneurship is closely linked with creativity and innovation. By fostering an entrepreneurial mindset, students are encouraged to think outside the box and develop innovative solutions to problems. Amabile et al. (1996) confirm that creativity is significantly enhanced in environments that support autonomy, challenge, and resource accessibility.

Steampreneurship effectively equips students with the skills necessary for success in the real world. These skills include critical thinking, collaboration, and adaptability—all of which are essential in navigating the complexities of a globalized society.

Inclusivity and Accessibility in Steampreneurship

Inclusivity and accessibility are central tenets of Steampreneurship, which aims to address and bridge educational disparities by providing diverse and equitable learning opportunities. This section highlights how Steampreneurship fosters an educational environment that is accessible to all students, regardless of their socio-economic background, cultural heritage, or learning capabilities, thereby promoting equity in education.

Addressing Educational Disparities

Universal Design for Learning (UDL): Steampreneurship incorporates principles of Universal Design for Learning, which involve creating course materials and teaching methods that are accessible to all students. UDL allows for multiple means of representation, expression, and engagement, ensuring that learning experiences are adaptable to meet the diverse needs of students. Research by Rose and Meyer (2002) on UDL shows that this approach significantly enhances engagement and understanding among a wide range of student populations, including those with disabilities.

Culturally Responsive Teaching: Steampreneurship values and incorporates students' cultural contexts into the learning process. This approach not only respects and acknowledges the importance of students' backgrounds but also enhances learning by making education more relevant and engaging. Ladson-Billings (1995) emphasizes that culturally responsive teaching effectively closes the gap in academic performance between students from different cultural backgrounds by utilizing cultural knowledge, prior experiences, and performance styles of diverse students to make learning more appropriate and effective.

Enhancing Access to Learning Opportunities

Technology Integration: Steampreneurship leverages technology to make learning more accessible. Online platforms, digital tools, and collaborative technologies ensure that students can access learning resources and participate in educational activities regardless of physical location. A study by Warschauer and Matuchniak (2010) points out that technology, when used appropriately, can significantly reduce barriers to education for students from underserved communities by providing them with access to information, tools for collaboration, and avenues for expression.

Flexible Learning Environments: By offering flexible learning environments and schedules, Steampreneurship helps accommodate students' diverse needs. This flexibility is particularly beneficial for students who may face challenges such as geographical constraints, family responsibilities, or different learning speeds. Asynchronicity in learning options allows students to engage with materials at their own pace, which is crucial for inclusive education.

Promoting Equity in Education

Equitable Assessment Practices: Steampreneurship employs assessment methods that are fair and accommodating to diverse learners. These assessments often include portfolios, presentations, and project-based tasks that allow students to demonstrate their knowledge and skills in various formats. Chappuis (2005) suggests that such inclusive assessment practices provide a more accurate representation of student learning and capabilities, promoting fairness and equity.

Community and Stakeholder Engagement: Steampreneurship encourages the involvement of community members and stakeholders in the learning process, which helps ensure that educational practices are relevant and supportive of the community's needs. This engagement is a critical aspect of inclusive education as it fosters a supportive network that values and advocates for all students' educational success.

Steampreneurship's commitment to inclusivity and accessibility ensures that all students have the opportunity to engage in meaningful and equitable educational experiences. By addressing disparities and promoting diverse learning approaches, Steampreneurship plays a pivotal role in advancing educational equity.

What Are We Waiting For?

As educators, administrators, and policymakers, you hold the keys to reshaping the educational experiences of future generations. The challenges of the modern world demand a robust, dynamic, and integrated approach to education—one that prepares students not just to meet the future but to shape it. Steampreneurship through Interdisciplinary Experiential Entrepreneurship offers a pathway forward, merging rigorous academic content with real-world application through interdisciplinary learning, experiential education, and entrepreneurship.

Integrate Steampreneurship into Curricula: I encourage you to consider the integration of Steampreneurship into your educational systems and policies. By adopting Steampreneurship, schools can transform traditional learning environments into vibrant hubs of creativity and innovation that engage and inspire both students and teachers alike. This transformation is not just about improving educational outcomes but about equipping young minds to tackle global challenges with confidence and ingenuity.

Policy Development: Policymakers should advocate for and support the adoption of Steampreneurshipby providing the necessary resources, training, and infrastructure. Investments in professional development for teachers, technology for classrooms, and partnerships with industries are critical steps in implementing Steampreneurshipeffectively.

Community Engagement: Engage with local communities and stakeholders to ensure that the Steampreneurship model addresses the unique needs and leverages the strengths of each community. This inclusive approach will not only enhance the relevance of education but also strengthen community ties and support systems.

Future Prospects

The future of Steampreneurshipin education is bright and brimming with possibilities. As we look forward, several emerging trends and technologies are set to enhance the implementation and impact of Steampreneurship:

Artificial Intelligence and Machine Learning: These technologies can personalize learning experiences and manage the complex data and interactions involved in interdisciplinary studies. AI can help tailor educational content to match students' learning paces and styles, making education more accessible and effective.

Virtual Reality and Augmented Reality: VR and AR can bring experiential learning to a new level by simulating real-world environments and scenarios that are otherwise inaccessible. For instance, students can virtually visit archaeological sites, simulate business markets, or explore different ecosystems, providing a depth of experience that enhances understanding and retention.

Global Learning Networks: Technology enables the creation of global classrooms where students from different parts of the world can collaborate on projects, share insights, and understand global perspectives firsthand. This exposure is invaluable in cultivating a truly global mindset.

Sustainability and Social Responsibility: As global issues like climate change and social equity remain at the forefront, Steampreneurshipprograms will increasingly need to integrate these themes. Teaching students to develop sustainable, socially responsible solutions to real-world problems will be crucial in shaping future leaders and innovators.

To educators, administrators, and policymakers, the call to action is clear: embrace Steampreneurshipto foster an education system that is fit for the future. Let us prepare our students not just to navigate the world but to improve it, equipping them with the skills, knowledge, and ethical grounding they need to lead with confidence and compassion.

The evolution of Steampreneurship is not just an educational imperative but a global necessity. As we advance, let us ensure that our educational practices are as dynamic and interconnected as the world our students will inherit. Embrace Steampreneurship, and let us together turn educational challenges into opportunities for growth, innovation, and global leadership.

GLOBAL AWARENESS IN EDUCATION

Understanding Global Markets

Teaching Global Economic Literacy

In an era defined by globalization, understanding global markets is crucial for students to fully grasp the economic forces that shape our world. Steampreneurship strategically integrates lessons on global economics, supply chains, and international trade into its curriculum, emphasizing the interconnectedness of global markets and the impact on daily life and business operations.

Integration into Curriculum: Steampreneurship introduces students to global economic concepts through an integrated curriculum where economics is not taught in isolation but as part of a broader interdisciplinary framework. For instance, students may explore the economics of climate change by examining international agreements and their economic impacts alongside scientific data on environmental effects, thus seeing firsthand the interplay between economics, environmental science, and policy.

Supply Chain Dynamics: Supply chains are a vital component of global economics, illustrating the complexity of global trade and its relevance to everyday products. Through case studies, such as the production and distribution of smartphones or clothing, students learn how raw materials and products move across continents, involving numerous economic, political, and social factors. This understanding helps students appreciate the scale and complexity of global trade and the vulnerabilities within these supply chains, as evidenced by disruptions like those seen during the COVID-19 pandemic (Ivanov, 2020).

Real-World Applications and Simulations: Steampreneurship utilizes simulations to teach international trade and economics. These simulations allow students to role-play as country representatives, business owners, or international negotiators, making decisions that affect simulated economic outcomes. This active learning strategy enhances students' understanding of economic principles and their applications in real-world scenarios, fostering a deeper comprehension of global economic dynamics (Carpenter, 2018).

Assessment of Global Market Understanding: To assess students' grasp of global markets, Steampreneurship employs project-based evaluations where students analyze specific markets or create business plans that respond to global economic conditions. This approach not only tests theoretical knowledge but also students' ability to apply this knowledge in practical, economically sound projects.

By integrating global economic literacy into its core curriculum, Steampreneurship equips students with a deep understanding of how global markets operate and how they are influenced by and influence other sectors. This knowledge is crucial for developing informed, capable individuals who can navigate and contribute to the global economy effectively.

Real-World Examples and Case Studies

To enhance understanding of global markets, Steampreneurship incorporates a range of case studies that showcase how businesses operate across diverse geopolitical landscapes. These examples illuminate the impact of global economic policies on local economies and provide students with insights into the complexities of international business operations.

Case Study 1: Multinational Corporations (MNCs) and Local Impact

Example: Toyota's Global Production Strategy

Toyota, a Japanese multinational automaker, has manufacturing plants in over 27 countries and regions. Through a case study on Toyota's strategy, students explore how Toyota adapts to local market conditions and regulatory environments. This case study highlights Toyota's use of a 'global-local' strategy, where core operations are standardized globally, while some aspects are adapted to meet local tastes and comply with local regulations (Liker & Choi, 2004).

Educational Focus: This case study teaches students about the balance between global standardization and local adaptation, a critical strategy for international businesses.

Case Study 2: The Impact of Trade Policies on Local Economies

Example: The North American Free Trade Agreement (NAFTA)

By examining NAFTA, students assess the effects of this significant trade agreement between Canada, the United States, and Mexico on local industries such as agriculture and automotive manufacturing. The renegotiation to the United States-Mexico-Canada Agreement (USMCA) provides a contemporary angle to understand how economic policies evolve.

Educational Focus: This analysis helps students understand how international trade agreements can boost economic growth or lead to job losses and industry decline in certain sectors, depending on the terms and conditions of the agreement (Villarreal & Fergusson, 2020).

Case Study 3: International Supply Chain Management

Example: Apple Inc.'s Supply Chain

A study of Apple Inc.'s supply chain demonstrates the complexity of managing operations across multiple countries, particularly in Asia. Students explore how Apple coordinates with hundreds of suppliers from various countries to assemble products like the iPhone, and the logistical and ethical challenges involved (Khan, Alam, & Alam, 2015).

Educational Focus: This case study highlights issues of supply chain resilience, ethical sourcing, and the strategic placement of production facilities.

Case Study 4: Small Business Global Expansion
Example: Craft Brewery International Expansion

Small businesses increasingly participate in global markets. A case study on a U.S.-based craft brewery expanding into European markets illustrates challenges smaller enterprises face, such as scaling production, understanding foreign consumer behavior, and navigating local laws.

Educational Focus: This case demonstrates the importance of cultural competence and market research in successfully introducing products to new international markets.

These case studies are vital components of Steampreneurship, providing students with concrete examples of how theoretical knowledge is applied in real-world settings. They not only illustrate the intricacies of international business operations but also encourage students to think critically about the broader implications of business decisions on global and local scales.

Simulations and Role-Playing: Enhancing Understanding of Global Markets

Simulations and role-playing exercises are dynamic educational tools used extensively in Steampreneurship (Steampreneurship) to teach complex concepts such as international trade dynamics, currency exchange, and global market trends. These interactive methods allow students to experience the nuances of global economics firsthand, promoting a deeper understanding through active participation.

The Role of Simulations in Learning

Immersive Learning Environments: Simulations create immersive environments where students can engage with economic models and global market scenarios in a controlled, yet realistic setting. By acting out roles as business leaders, government officials, or international traders, students encounter the challenges and opportunities that real-world professionals face in the global marketplace.

Understanding Complexity: Through simulations, students can see the immediate consequences of economic decisions, such as adjusting interest rates, imposing tariffs, or negotiating trade deals. These exercises help students understand how such decisions ripple through global markets, affecting everything from currency values to job creation. Research by Faria et al. (2009) found that simulations enhance the comprehension of complex subjects by allowing students to experiment with economic strategies and witness the outcomes in real-time.

Benefits of Role-Playing

Development of Soft Skills: Role-playing exercises cultivate essential soft skills such as negotiation, communication, and strategic thinking. As students take on different personas and navigate various economic scenarios, they learn to articulate their views, persuade others, and forge agreements under pressure. These are invaluable skills in the realm of international business and trade.

Empathy and Perspective-Taking: Role-playing also encourages students to consider perspectives other than their own, fostering empathy and a better understanding of the diverse stakeholders in global economics. This can be particularly enlightening when students represent countries with differing economic priorities and challenges, as noted by Wright-Maley (2015), who emphasizes the role of perspective-taking in deepening students' understanding of global issues.

Implementing Effective Simulations

Design and Preparation: For simulations to be effective, they must be well-designed and include realistic scenarios that accurately reflect the complexities of the global economy. Educators need to prepare these simulations with clear objectives, detailed backgrounds for roles, and scenarios that are grounded in current global economic conditions.

Debriefing: Perhaps the most critical component of simulations and role-playing exercises is the debriefing session. After the simulation, educators should guide students through a reflective discussion on what they learned, what strategies succeeded or failed, and how these lessons apply to real-world economic contexts. Debriefing helps consolidate learning and ensures students can transfer these insights into their academic and future professional lives.

Simulations and role-playing are powerful methods within Steampreneurship to teach the dynamic and often complex principles of international trade and economics. By immersing students in realistic scenarios, these exercises not only enhance academic understanding but also develop practical skills that are crucial in a globalized world.

Cultural Competence

Integrating Cultural Studies

In the framework of Steampreneurship through Interdisciplinary Experiential Entrepreneurship, cultural studies are not isolated within a specific domain but are seamlessly integrated across all subjects. This approach is designed to cultivate a deep understanding of global diversity and enhance students' ability to function in an interconnected world.

Comprehensive Cultural Integration: Steampreneurship incorporates cultural perspectives into every part of the curriculum to ensure that students gain a comprehensive understanding of the world's diverse social, economic, and political landscapes. For instance, in mathematics classes, students might explore the development of number systems in ancient civilizations; in science, they could study contributions from various cultures to modern technology and medicine.

Real-World Application: Steampreneurship emphasizes the application of cultural knowledge in real-world contexts. This includes collaborative projects that involve international communication and problem-solving with peers from different cultural backgrounds. These activities encourage students to apply their cultural knowledge practically and develop skills that are critical in global citizenship.

Enhancing Global Literacy

Cultural Case Studies: Steampreneurship uses case studies from a variety of cultures to illustrate how societal issues can have global implications. For example, students might examine how different cultures address public health, environmental sustainability, or education, thereby understanding that these challenges, while universal, are approached in culturally specific ways.

Guest Speakers and Cultural Exchanges: Bringing in experts from various fields and cultures, as well as organizing virtual or physical exchange programs, enriches students' learning experiences. These interactions allow students to engage directly with diverse cultural narratives and perspectives, enhancing their empathy and understanding.

Multilingual Education: Understanding language is crucial to understanding culture. Steampreneurship promotes multilingual education, encouraging students to learn and use second or third languages. This linguistic capability is fundamental in appreciating cultural nuances and fosters more effective communication in a globalized economy.

Developing Empathy and Understanding

Empathy and cross-cultural understanding are crucial skills in today's globalized world. Steampreneurship through Interdisciplinary Experiential Entrepreneurship incorporates specific strategies designed to enhance these competencies among students. This section outlines how Steampreneurship uses exchange programs, collaborative international projects, and multimedia resources to deepen students' appreciation for and understanding of diverse cultures.

Exchange Programs

Global Immersion Experiences: Exchange programs are a cornerstone of Steampreneurship 's strategy to foster cultural empathy. By living and studying in a different country, students immerse themselves in the local culture, which helps them gain a profound understanding of and appreciation for that culture. This direct exposure challenges preconceptions and allows students to experience daily life from a different cultural perspective.

Partner Schools Collaboration: Steampreneurship encourages partnerships with schools across the globe, enabling students to participate in exchange programs that are both physical and virtual. This collaboration extends the classroom walls internationally, giving students the opportunity to interact with peers from diverse backgrounds on a regular basis. Research by Williams (2005) highlights that such immersion and interaction significantly improve students' cultural sensitivity and empathy.

Collaborative International Projects

Team-Based Global Learning Initiatives: Collaborative projects involve students from different countries working together to solve real-world problems. These projects help students understand the global implications of local actions and vice versa. For example, a project might involve students from different parts of the world coming together to address climate change, exploring how different regions are affected by and respond to this global issue.

Technology-Enabled Communication: Modern technology platforms facilitate these international collaborations, allowing for regular interaction and sharing of ideas across borders. Students use tools like video conferencing, shared digital workspaces, and social media to communicate and work together, enhancing their ability to navigate cultural differences and build mutual respect (O'Dowd, 2013).

Multimedia Resources

Cultural Representation in Media: Steampreneurship utilizes films, documentaries, music, and art from around the world as educational resources. These media are used not only to impart knowledge but also to stimulate discussion about cultural norms, values, and issues, helping students develop a nuanced understanding of the cultures they study.

Interactive Cultural Simulations: Advanced simulations and virtual reality (VR) experiences allow students to engage in cultural scenarios that they might not otherwise encounter. These simulations can range from navigating a busy street in a foreign city to participating in a cultural ceremony, providing immersive experiences that build empathy and understanding (Godwin-Jones, 2014).

Developing empathy and understanding across cultures is more than an educational goal—it's a necessity for fostering global citizens capable of respectful and effective interaction in a diverse world. The strategies implemented in Steampreneurship not only educate but also transform students, equipping them with the empathy and skills needed to thrive in a multicultural environment.

Assessing Cultural Competence

Reflective Essays and Portfolios: Students are encouraged to write reflective essays and maintain portfolios that document their cultural learning journeys. These assessments help educators track students' progress in understanding and valuing cultural diversity.

Performance-Based Assessments: Performances, presentations, and group projects can serve as dynamic methods to assess cultural understanding. For example, students might present research on the business practices of a particular region or create multimedia projects that explore cultural heritage.

Peer Feedback: Peer assessments in group projects can provide insight into how students collaborate across cultural lines. Feedback from classmates can help students refine their approach to intercultural interactions.

Integrating cultural studies across all subjects helps prepare students to navigate and contribute positively to a culturally diverse world. Steampreneurship 's approach to cultural competence not only educates but also empowers students, giving them the tools they need to engage with and respect an array of cultural perspectives.

Assessing Cultural Competence

Cultural competence is a critical component of global education, empowering students to interact effectively and respectfully across cultural boundaries. Steampreneurship through Interdisciplinary Experiential Entrepreneurship places a strong emphasis on not only teaching about diverse cultures but also on developing the practical skills needed for effective cross-cultural interaction. This section discusses methodologies for assessing students' cultural competence, which is pivotal for ensuring that these educational goals are met effectively.

Tools for Assessing Cultural Competence

Simulations and Role-Playing Exercises: One effective way to assess cultural competence is through simulations and role-playing exercises that mimic cross-cultural interactions. These activities can help educators evaluate students' abilities to navigate and respond to cultural nuances in real-time. Such assessments are often more dynamic and reflective of students' actual capabilities than traditional tests or written exams.

Reflective Journals: Encouraging students to keep journals during courses involving cultural studies can provide insights into their understanding and personal growth regarding cultural competence. Educators can assess these journals for evidence of reflection on cultural interactions, changes in perspectives, and the application of cultural knowledge in various contexts (Schön, 1983).

Portfolios: A portfolio that collects diverse artifacts from a student's coursework, such as essays, project reports, and multimedia projects, can be used to assess growth in cultural competence over time. Portfolios allow educators to evaluate not just the factual knowledge students have acquired but also their ability to apply this knowledge in culturally sensitive ways (Barrett, 2000).

Peer Feedback and Group Evaluations: Since much of cultural competence is demonstrated through interaction, peer feedback and group evaluations during group projects can be invaluable. These assessments can provide insights into how students handle cross-cultural teamwork and communication, critical components of cultural competence.

Frameworks for Measuring Cultural Competence

Developmental Model of Intercultural Sensitivity (DMIS): The DMIS, developed by Bennett (1993), is a theoretical framework that outlines the different stages of becoming culturally competent, from denial to integration. Educators can use this model to assess where students are in their cultural competence development and to provide targeted interventions to help them progress.

Intercultural Development Inventory (IDI): The IDI is a well-validated tool for assessing intercultural competence that has been used in various educational and corporate settings. It provides a measure of an individual's capability to deal with cultural differences, offering detailed feedback that can help educators tailor their instructional approaches (Hammer, 2011).

Cultural Intelligence Scale: This scale measures an individual's capability to function effectively in culturally diverse settings. It assesses four dimensions: cognitive, metacognitive, motivational, and behavioral, each critical for effective cultural interaction (Earley & Ang, 2003).

Assessing cultural competence requires a multifaceted approach that considers cognitive understanding, emotional engagement, and behavioral skills. By employing a combination of these assessment tools and methodologies, educators in a Steampreneurship framework can ensure that students are not only knowledgeable about other cultures but are also adept at navigating and respecting these differences in real-world settings.

Technology's Role in Global Education

Bridging Local and Global Learning Environments

The role of digital tools and technology is pivotal in Steampreneurship, especially when it comes to bridging the gap between local and global educational experiences. By harnessing the power of modern technology, Steampreneurship connects students with their peers around the world, facilitating an exchange of ideas and perspectives that enriches the learning experience and fosters a more comprehensive understanding of global issues.

Enhancing Connectivity Through Digital Platforms

Virtual Classrooms and Collaborative Tools: Tools such as video conferencing software, online forums, and collaborative platforms like Google Classroom and Microsoft Teams enable real-time interactions between students from different geographical locations. These technologies allow for the seamless exchange of ideas and foster collaborative learning projects across borders. According to research by Martin and Ertzberger (2016), virtual classrooms and collaborative tools not only enhance communication and collaboration but also improve student engagement and learning outcomes by providing access to a wider range of perspectives and expertise.

Social Media as a Learning Tool: Social media platforms like Twitter, Facebook, and Instagram are increasingly used in educational contexts to connect students with global learning communities. These platforms support the sharing of cultural experiences and academic knowledge, extending learning beyond traditional classroom boundaries. A study by Greenhow and Lewin (2016) highlights the potential of social media to facilitate meaningful connections and discussions among students from diverse cultural backgrounds, thus enriching their educational experience.

Facilitating Global Interaction

Language Translation Technologies: Advances in language translation technology, such as Google Translate and real-time translation apps, have significantly lowered language barriers that once impeded international collaboration. These technologies enable students to communicate effectively with peers in different countries, making collaborative projects more accessible and productive. Research by O'Hagan and Ashworth (2013) discusses the role of translation technology in promoting inclusivity and participation in global educational projects.

Interactive Learning Environments: Tools like virtual reality (VR) and augmented reality (AR) provide immersive learning experiences that can simulate real-world environments from around the globe. For example, students can take virtual field trips to historical sites, natural wonders, or museums in different countries, gaining experiential knowledge that would be difficult to convey through traditional teaching methods. Guttentag (2010) notes that VR and AR can dramatically enhance the realism of educational simulations, providing students with a deeper, more engaging learning experience.

Digital tools and technology are integral to the Steampreneurship framework, transforming traditional education by connecting local learning environments with global contexts. This integration not only enhances educational accessibility and engagement but also prepares students to succeed in a globally interconnected world.

Enhancing Access and Participation

The integration of online platforms, virtual classrooms, and digital collaboration tools in Steampreneurship through Steampreneurship through Steampreneurship through Steampreneurship through Steampreneurship through Steampreneurship through Steampreneurship (Steampreneurship) plays a pivotal role in enhancing educational access and promoting inclusive participation. These technologies break down geographic, economic, and social barriers, enabling students from various parts of the world to engage with global learning communities and benefit from diverse educational resources.

Leveraging Online Platforms for Broader Access

Global Reach of Online Education: Online platforms such as Coursera, EdX, and Khan Academy offer courses from institutions around the world, making high-quality education accessible to anyone with an internet connection. These platforms democratize access to learning, allowing students from remote or underserved regions to partake in courses offered by top universities, which would otherwise be inaccessible to them. Research by Zhu et al. (2020) emphasizes how online learning platforms can significantly increase educational outreach, providing learning opportunities regardless of geographical constraints.

Customizable Learning Experiences: Online education is not only accessible but also customizable to different learning needs and styles. Students can learn at their own pace, review content as needed, and choose from a plethora of courses that match their interests and career goals. This level of customization fosters a more inclusive learning environment that caters to diverse student populations, including those with disabilities or other specific needs.

Virtual Classrooms Enhancing Interaction

Interactive Learning Environment: Virtual classrooms replicate the interactive aspects of traditional classrooms in a digital environment. Tools like Zoom, Microsoft Teams, and Google Meet enable real-time video communications, where students can participate in lectures, engage in group discussions, and work collaboratively on projects, regardless of their physical location. The study by Bower et al. (2015) found that interactive technologies in virtual classrooms could enhance student engagement and collaboration, making learning more dynamic and effective.

Incorporation of Collaborative Tools: Digital collaboration tools such as Slack, Asana, and Trello facilitate project management and teamwork among students scattered across the globe. These tools support task scheduling, progress tracking, and real-time feedback, which are essential for managing group projects and fostering a sense of community among distant learners.

Digital Tools Bridging Cultural Gaps

Cross-Cultural Exchanges: Digital tools also facilitate cross-cultural exchanges by connecting students with peers in different countries. Through structured activities like global virtual teams and international online forums, students explore cultural differences and similarities, enhancing their global awareness and intercultural competence. As posited by O'Dowd (2013), such virtual exchanges are invaluable for developing students' abilities to navigate and appreciate diverse cultural landscapes.

Technological Literacy: The use of digital tools in education also enhances students' technological literacy, an essential skill in today's digital world. By regularly using these tools, students become proficient in digital communication and information management, skills that are increasingly important in both academic and professional settings.

Online platforms, virtual classrooms, and digital collaboration tools have transformed educational landscapes, making learning more accessible, inclusive, and adaptable to the needs of a diverse student body. These technologies not only facilitate access to education but also enhance the quality and scope of learning experiences.

Future Technologies in Global Education

Emerging technologies such as artificial intelligence (AI) and blockchain are set to profoundly transform global education. These technologies offer the potential to enhance personalization and ensure the integrity of educational credentials, thereby addressing some of the key challenges in current educational models. This section explores how AI and blockchain could revolutionize the educational landscape, making learning more adaptive, inclusive, and secure.

Artificial Intelligence (AI) in Education

Personalized Learning Experiences: AI can significantly enhance the personalization of learning by analyzing individual learning patterns and adapting instructional materials accordingly. AI systems can provide real-time feedback to students, tailor educational content to their learning pace and style, and even predict and address their individual needs. Zhou et al. (2020) discuss how AI-driven adaptive learning systems have the potential to transform traditional education by delivering a highly personalized learning experience that can improve student engagement and outcomes.

Automated Administrative Tasks: AI can also automate administrative tasks such as grading, attendance tracking, and responses to common student inquiries, which can free up educators to focus more on teaching and less on bureaucratic aspects. This shift can lead to more efficient classroom management and enhanced interactions between teachers and students.

Blockchain for Educational Integrity

Secure Credentialing: Blockchain technology offers a robust solution to the challenge of verifying educational credentials. By creating tamper-proof digital ledgers for storing educational certificates and achievements, blockchain ensures the integrity and portability of credentials. This technology can make the process of credential verification simpler and faster, which is crucial in a global educational context where students often move across borders. Sharples and Domingue (2016) highlight blockchain's potential to secure academic credentials and provide a transparent record that is accessible across different institutions and countries.

Facilitating Lifelong Learning: Blockchain can also support lifelong learning by enabling the accumulation and preservation of educational records from various institutions over a lifetime. This capability can assist in career development and continuous education, as learners compile a comprehensive, secure, and immutable record of their learning achievements.

Future Prospects

AI and Global Classroom Connectivity: Looking ahead, AI could play a pivotal role in enhancing global classroom connectivity by translating languages in real-time, thus facilitating seamless communication among students from different linguistic backgrounds. This technology could break down the final barriers in global education, ensuring that language is no longer an obstacle to international collaboration and learning.

Blockchain in Continuous Assessment: Blockchain could further be used to revolutionize assessment systems, where continuous and cumulative assessments are securely recorded and shared with relevant stakeholders. This approach could lead to more holistic and continuous evaluation methods that reflect a student's progress over time rather than through one-time examinations.

The integration of AI and blockchain into global education systems holds the promise of making learning more personalized, secure, and globally accessible. As these technologies continue to evolve, their potential to transform educational practices and administration represents a significant leap forward for educators and learners alike.

Implementing Global Awareness in Curricula

Curriculum Design

Incorporating global awareness into educational curricula is essential for preparing students to understand and engage effectively with the complex issues facing today's interconnected world. Designing a curriculum that integrates global awareness involves more than simply adding international content; it requires a comprehensive approach that infuses global perspectives throughout the educational experience. This section provides guidelines for developing curricula that foster a balanced and in-depth understanding of global issues.

Integrative Approach:

- **Interdisciplinary Themes:** Design curriculum units around global themes, such as sustainability, global health, and international relations, that require input from multiple disciplines. This approach helps students see the connections between subjects and understand how complex issues are interrelated.

- **Project-Based Learning:** Utilize project-based learning strategies that encourage students to research and respond to real-world global issues. This method promotes active learning and helps students apply theoretical knowledge in practical scenarios.

Cultural Inclusivity:

- **Diverse Perspectives:** Ensure that the curriculum includes multiple cultural perspectives. This can be achieved by incorporating literature, case studies, and examples from various countries and cultures.
- **Collaborative Learning:** Design activities that encourage students to work with peers from different cultural backgrounds, possibly through online collaboration tools. This exposure to diverse viewpoints enhances cultural understanding and empathy.

Skill Development:

- **Critical Thinking and Analysis:** Focus on developing students' ability to critically analyze global issues. Encourage them to consider and evaluate the impact of these issues from multiple viewpoints and to think about sustainable solutions.
- **Communication Skills:** Emphasize the importance of effective communication skills, including the ability to argue persuasively and respectfully and to listen to and consider diverse points of view.

Utilization of Technology:

- **Digital Tools:** Leverage technology to provide students with access to global information sources, virtual tours, and interactions with international experts. Tools such as video conferencing can connect classrooms with peers and teachers around the world, enhancing students' global awareness.
- **Online Platforms:** Use online learning platforms to offer modules on global issues, which can be updated regularly to reflect current events and emerging trends.

Assessment Strategies:

- **Reflective Assessments:** Incorporate reflective essays and journals where students can express their understanding of global issues and personal growth in global awareness.
- **Performance-Based Assessments:** Use presentations, debates, and group projects to assess students' ability to apply their knowledge of global issues in various communicative and practical contexts.

Research Support

Studies have shown that curricula with integrated global awareness components significantly enhance students' empathy, critical thinking, and readiness to engage with others in a globally interconnected world. According to research by Mansilla and Jackson (2011), students exposed to such curricula demonstrate a deeper understanding of global interdependencies and are better prepared to act as global citizens.

Professional Development for Educators

For educators to effectively impart global awareness and competencies to students, they require ongoing professional development that equips them with the necessary skills and knowledge. This section emphasizes the importance of professional development in helping educators teach global concepts effectively and adapt to the evolving educational demands of a globalized world.

Need for Specialized Training

Understanding Global Concepts: Educators must grasp complex global issues and understand diverse cultural perspectives to effectively teach these concepts. Professional development programs can provide teachers with up-to-date information on global events, international relations, and cultural studies, ensuring they have a solid foundation to support their teaching.

Integrative Teaching Methods: Training should also focus on pedagogical strategies that integrate global learning across curricula. This includes interdisciplinary teaching methods, project-based learning, and the use of technology to connect with classrooms around the world. Professional development can introduce educators to these methods and provide them with the tools to implement them effectively.

Components of Effective Professional Development

Workshops and Seminars: Regular workshops and seminars led by experts in global education can help teachers stay current with the latest research and trends in global issues. These sessions can also cover practical teaching strategies to engage students with complex international content.

Collaborative Learning Communities: Creating professional learning communities where educators can share resources and strategies is another critical aspect of professional development. These communities can be platforms for teachers to collaborate on lesson plans, discuss challenges they face in teaching global concepts, and share successes and innovations.

Study Abroad and Exchange Programs: Providing opportunities for teachers to participate in study abroad or teacher exchange programs can enhance their understanding of global contexts. These experiences allow educators to immerse themselves in different cultures, gaining insights and experiences that can enrich their teaching practices.

Online Training Modules: Online professional development courses can offer flexibility and accessibility for teachers seeking to enhance their knowledge and skills in global education. These modules can include interactive content, discussion forums, and case studies that allow teachers to learn at their own pace and apply what they learn directly to their teaching.

Research Support

Research underscores the importance of professional development in enabling effective teaching of global concepts. Darling-Hammond and McLaughlin (1995) argue that professional development that is collaborative, reflective, and integrated into daily practices is most likely to produce positive changes in teaching practice. Additionally, Longview Foundation (2008) highlights that teachers who receive targeted training in global education are more confident and effective in delivering global curriculum content.

Community and Parental Involvement

Involving the community and parents in global education initiatives is crucial for enhancing support and understanding of the program's benefits. This section explores how engaging these key stakeholders can deepen the impact of global education, ensuring a supportive environment that fosters an appreciation for cultural diversity and global interconnectedness.

Importance of Community Engagement

Resource Sharing and Support: Community organizations, local businesses, and cultural institutions can provide resources that enrich global education programs. By partnering with these entities, schools can offer students authentic learning experiences that extend beyond the classroom. Community involvement also helps in garnering support for global education initiatives, as stakeholders see direct benefits to local development.

Enhancing Cultural Programs: Communities with diverse cultural representations can serve as invaluable resources for authentic cultural exchanges. Programs that involve local cultural groups in school activities can provide students with firsthand experiences of different cultures, enhancing their understanding and appreciation.

Role of Parental Involvement

Enhancing Learning at Home: Parents play a crucial role in reinforcing the concepts learned in school. When they are involved and informed about the global education curriculum, they can better support their children's learning at home, discuss global issues, and provide encouragement. This continued engagement at home helps solidify students' learning experiences and fosters an environment where global awareness is continuously emphasized.

Building Support for Global Initiatives: Educating parents about the importance of global competence can help build a foundation of support for these initiatives. Workshops, information sessions, and parent-teacher meetings can be used to explain the skills students gain from global education and how these skills are applicable in today's interconnected world.

Strategies for Effective Involvement

Community and Parent Workshops: Regular workshops that include parents and community members can be effective in communicating the goals and benefits of global education.

These workshops can serve to educate about global competencies, cultural diversity, and the economic and social advantages of a globally aware educational program.

Volunteer Opportunities: Creating volunteer opportunities for parents and community members in global education activities can increase engagement and investment. Volunteers can share their expertise and experiences related to global business, cultural practices, or international travel, enriching the curriculum.

Collaborative Projects: Schools can design projects that require students to work with community members or organizations, thereby solving real-world problems while utilizing global perspectives. These projects not only enhance learning but also strengthen community ties.

Research Support

Research indicates that community and parental involvement are key factors in the success of educational programs. According to Epstein (2011), when schools, families, and communities work together, student outcomes improve, and schools get better. Henderson and Mapp (2002) also found strong correlations between family involvement and student success in school, including higher academic achievement.

Challenges and Opportunities

Integrating global awareness into education is a vital step toward preparing students for the interconnected world of the 21st century. However, this integration presents several challenges that need to be addressed to effectively implement and sustain such initiatives. This section discusses these challenges along with potential solutions and opportunities for enhancing global education.

Addressing Challenges

Resource Limitations:

- *Challenge:* Schools often face budget constraints and limited resources, which can hinder the implementation of comprehensive global education programs that require new materials, technologies, and training.
- *Solution:* Schools can seek partnerships with local businesses and international organizations that have an interest in promoting global awareness. Grant programs and educational foundations are also potential sources of

funding. Collaborative programs with other schools, both nationally and internationally, can share resources and reduce costs.

Resistance to Change:

- *Challenge:* Educators and administrators may resist integrating global awareness due to the comfort with existing curricula or skepticism about the relevance of global education.

- *Solution:* Professional development programs that clearly demonstrate the benefits of global education and provide practical strategies for integration can help overcome resistance. Highlighting successful case studies and facilitating discussions with educators who have effectively implemented such programs can also mitigate apprehension.

Biases in Content:

- *Challenge:* There is a risk of cultural bias in the content used for teaching global awareness, which can lead to a skewed understanding of different cultures and global issues.

- *Solution:* Curricula should be designed with input from a diverse group of educators and experts to ensure a balanced perspective. Regular reviews and updates of educational materials are essential to address and correct any biases. Incorporating a variety of sources and perspectives, including primary sources from different countries, can enhance content diversity.

Exploiting Opportunities

Technology in Global Education:

- *Opportunity:* Digital tools and online platforms provide unprecedented opportunities to access diverse resources and connect with people around the world.
- *Application:* Utilize online platforms for virtual exchanges and collaborations with students and educators from different countries. Implementing technologies such as VR for virtual field trips can provide immersive experiences that are otherwise not possible.

Interdisciplinary Learning:

- *Opportunity:* Global awareness naturally lends itself to interdisciplinary teaching, which can enrich students' learning experiences and understanding of complex global issues.
- *Application:* Design projects and assignments that require students to apply knowledge from multiple disciplines, thereby fostering a deeper understanding and appreciation of how global issues are interconnected.

Community Engagement:

- *Opportunity:* Engaging with local immigrant communities and international organizations can provide authentic experiences and resources for learning about global cultures and issues.
- *Application:* Organize community events, guest lectures, and cultural fairs that involve both students and the community. These activities can serve as both educational tools and ways to strengthen community ties.

Research Support

Studies have shown that overcoming these challenges can significantly enhance students' readiness to participate effectively in the global community. According to Mansilla and Jackson (2011), students who receive a global education are better equipped to handle the complexities of modern global issues and are more empathetic towards other cultures.

Capitalizing on Opportunities: The Advantages of a Globally Aware Educational Framework

Incorporating global awareness into educational frameworks not only prepares students to navigate a complex world but also offers substantial benefits that can enhance their personal, academic, and professional lives. This section highlights how a globally aware educational framework can provide opportunities for improved employability, enhanced cultural sensitivity, and a more robust ability to address and understand global issues.

Improved Employability

Global Skill Set: In today's interconnected global economy, employers increasingly value candidates with a broad understanding of global markets, international regulations, and cross-cultural communication. A globally aware education equips students with these skills, making them more competitive and adaptable in the job market. According to a report by the British Council (2013), graduates with international experience and education are more likely to find employment quickly and to earn higher salaries than their peers without such backgrounds.

Adaptability in Various Sectors: Understanding global dynamics is beneficial not only in international business or politics but across all sectors, including technology, healthcare, and education, which are becoming increasingly globalized. This adaptability opens multiple career paths and broadens employment opportunities for students.

Enhanced Cultural Sensitivity

Interpersonal Skills: A globally aware curriculum fosters greater empathy and respect for other cultures, which are crucial interpersonal skills in both personal and professional contexts. Studies by Ang et al. (2007) have shown that individuals with higher cultural sensitivity are better able to navigate and succeed in diverse environments. These skills help in managing international teams, negotiating across cultures, and resolving conflicts in a culturally informed manner.

Inclusive Perspectives: Education that includes multiple cultural perspectives helps students recognize and challenge cultural biases, leading to more inclusive viewpoints. This inclusivity is essential for effective leadership and teamwork in today's diverse world.

Stronger Ability to Navigate Global Issues

Informed Decision-Making: Students educated in a globally aware framework are better equipped to understand and analyze complex global issues such as climate change, economic crises, and international conflicts. This understanding enables them to participate more effectively in discussions and decision-making processes about these issues, whether in their communities or in broader forums.

Proactive Global Citizenship: With a deep understanding of global interdependencies, students are more likely to engage in activities that promote global well-being, such as advocacy, volunteering, and policy-making. This proactive approach to global citizenship can lead to significant contributions to global challenges.

Research Support

Research consistently supports the benefits of global education. A study by Hunter et al. (2006) found that students who had engaged in an international curriculum exhibited enhanced global competence and self-confidence in their ability to understand and influence global systems and issues.

The Imperative for Global Awareness

As we conclude this exploration into the integration of global awareness into education, it becomes increasingly clear that preparing students for the complexities of a globalized world is not merely beneficial but essential. The dynamic interplay of cultures, economies, and technologies across borders defines our modern era. Educators, administrators, and policymakers must therefore prioritize and advocate for educational strategies that embed global awareness at the heart of learning experiences.

Necessity in a Globalized World

The world today is more interconnected than ever before. Economic, environmental, and social issues transcend local and national boundaries, requiring a nuanced understanding of global systems and interdependencies. Education systems that embrace global awareness equip students not only with the knowledge to understand these complexities but also with the critical thinking skills necessary to address them. This preparation is crucial for fostering a generation that can navigate global challenges with insight and empathy.

Embracing Comprehensive Global Education Strategies

A comprehensive global education strategy is not just about adding international content to the curriculum; it involves cultivating an educational ethos that values diversity, supports intercultural communication, and promotes global thinking. It requires continuous effort to ensure that these values are integrated into every aspect of educational planning and delivery.

By fostering global awareness in education, we prepare students to become competent, compassionate leaders who understand the importance of cultural sensitivity and global stewardship. These students are better equipped to make positive contributions in a world where global challenges require cooperative, innovative solutions.

The imperative for integrating global awareness into education cannot be overstated. It is a critical step toward not only enhancing individual educational outcomes but also toward building a more informed, empathetic, and proactive global citizenry. Let us embrace and advocate for these changes, ensuring that our educational systems evolve to meet the demands of an increasingly interconnected global community.

~ 4 ~

ENTREPRENEURSHIP AS A LEARNING TOOL

Basics of Business Education

Integrating Core Concepts

Entrepreneurship education integrates essential business knowledge by embedding fundamental economic principles directly into the learning framework. This section examines how concepts such as supply and demand, market structures, and economic cycles are intricately woven into the curriculum, providing students with a robust foundation in business understanding that is crucial for their future roles as entrepreneurs and innovators.

Economic Principles:

Supply and Demand: Understanding the dynamics of supply and demand is critical for any entrepreneurial venture. Students learn how prices are determined in the market and how these fundamental principles affect business decisions and strategies. Classroom simulations often involve scenarios where students must adjust their business operations based on changes in supply and demand, fostering a practical understanding of these concepts.

Market Structures: The curriculum explores different market structures—such as perfect competition, monopolistic competition, oligopoly, and monopoly—and their implications for business strategy and consumer behavior. Students analyze how these structures influence pricing, quality of goods and services, and the level of innovation within industries.

Economic Cycles: Students are taught to understand and anticipate economic cycles, enabling them to better prepare for economic downturns and capitalize on booms. Lessons focus on the indicators of economic health, such as GDP growth rates, unemployment levels, and consumer confidence, and how these factors can impact a business environment.

Application Through Case Studies and Simulations: Incorporating real-world case studies and simulations enhances students' understanding of economic principles by placing them in the context of actual business challenges. For example, a case study might involve a tech startup navigating a rapidly changing market, or a simulation might have students manage a virtual company through different economic cycles.

Incorporating Business Ethics: Understanding economic principles also involves recognizing the ethical dimensions of business decisions. Discussions on ethics are integrated into lessons on economic principles to ensure that students can identify and navigate the ethical implications of business strategies, such as pricing fairness, competition, and market manipulation.

Research Support:

Studies have shown that a solid grasp of basic economic principles enhances students' ability to make informed business decisions and contributes to successful entrepreneurial ventures. According to a report by the Network for Teaching Entrepreneurship (NFTE), students who receive entrepreneurship education are more adept at opportunity recognition and more resilient in adjusting their business models to economic realities (Network for Teaching Entrepreneurship, 2019).

Business Ethics in Entrepreneurship Education

Importance of Ethics in Business Education

Incorporating ethics into business education is crucial for preparing students to navigate the complex moral and ethical issues they will encounter in the business world. Ethics education teaches students not just about the mechanics of business but also about the responsibilities that come with running a business, including the implications of their decisions on society, the environment, and the economy.

Corporate Social Responsibility (CSR):

Understanding CSR: Students learn about the concept of Corporate Social Responsibility, which emphasizes that businesses have duties that extend beyond their shareholders to other stakeholders, including employees, communities, and the environment.

Application in Business: Through case studies and real-world examples, students explore how companies integrate CSR into their business models, examining the benefits and challenges of such integration. They learn how effective CSR strategies can improve a company's reputation, enhance customer loyalty, and contribute to its long-term success.

Ethical Decision-Making:

Frameworks and Approaches: Students are introduced to various ethical frameworks and decision-making models that help them analyze and resolve ethical dilemmas. These include consequentialist theories (focusing on the outcomes of decisions), deontological theories (focusing on duties and rules), and virtue ethics (focusing on the moral character of the decision-maker).

Practical Exercises: Simulations and role-playing exercises are used to put students in scenarios where they must make tough ethical choices, helping them to apply theoretical knowledge in a practical setting and see the real-world consequences of their decisions.

Impact of Business Activities:

Societal and Environmental Impacts: Students discuss case studies that highlight both positive and negative impacts of business activities on society and the environment. This includes examining cases of companies that have either successfully reduced their environmental footprint or faced backlash due to unethical practices.

Sustainability: The curriculum emphasizes the importance of sustainable business practices. Students learn how businesses can contribute to sustainable development by innovating new products and services that benefit society while minimizing environmental damage.

Research Support

The inclusion of ethics in business education has been shown to significantly enhance students' moral reasoning abilities and their likelihood of behaving ethically in their professional lives. According to a study by Bebeau and Thoma (2003), ethics education can effectively improve moral development in young adults, better preparing them for ethical challenges in the workplace.

Entrepreneurial Skills in Entrepreneurship Education

Entrepreneurship education is not only about instilling knowledge but also about developing critical entrepreneurial skills that enable students to launch and manage successful business ventures. This section explores essential entrepreneurial skills such as opportunity recognition, risk assessment, and resource management, and how these skills are taught and cultivated through entrepreneurship education.

Opportunity Recognition

Skill Development:
Conceptual Understanding: Students learn to identify market gaps and consumer needs that can be transformed into business opportunities. This skill is developed through the study of market trends, consumer behavior, and innovation techniques.

Practical Application: Through case studies, students analyze how successful entrepreneurs have identified and capitalized on opportunities. Workshops and brainstorming sessions are also used to practice these skills in a controlled environment.

Research Support: A study by Baron and Ensley (2006) emphasizes that the ability to recognize opportunities is a distinct skill that can be developed through targeted education and practice. This skill is critical because it sets the stage for the creation of new ventures and innovative solutions.

Risk Assessment

Skill Development:
Understanding Risk Types: Students are taught to categorize different types of risks, including financial, market, and operational risks. Understanding these distinctions is crucial for effective risk management.

Risk Mitigation Strategies: Education programs focus on strategies to assess and mitigate risks, such as diversification, insurance, and contingency planning. Role-playing and simulation games often help students apply these concepts in hypothetical business scenarios.

Research Support: Research by Sarasvathy (2001) on what makes entrepreneurs entrepreneurial highlights that skilled entrepreneurs often engage in what is called 'effectuation,' a process that includes understanding and managing risk through flexible strategies and leveraging unexpected opportunities.

Resource Management

Skill Development:

Resource Identification and Allocation: Students learn how to identify key resources necessary for business operations, including human, financial, and physical resources. They also practice allocating these resources efficiently to support business growth and sustainability.

Sustainable Practices: Modern entrepreneurship education increasingly stresses the importance of managing resources sustainably. This not only involves economic sustainability but also environmental and social stewardship.

Research Support: A study by Hockerts and Wüstenhagen (2010) illustrates that effective resource management is critical for the sustainability of startups. It ensures that new ventures can not only survive initial challenges but also scale up operations in a sustainable manner.

Project-Based Learning

Real-World Application: Business Scenario Simulations

Project-based learning (PBL) is a core component of entrepreneurship education, offering students practical, hands-on experiences through simulations that mimic real business challenges. This approach not only engages students but also deepens their understanding of what it takes to operate a successful business in today's competitive environment.

Business Scenario Simulations:

Starting a New Company:

Students are tasked with creating a business from the ground up, which involves conducting market research, defining a target audience, developing a product or service, and crafting a business plan. This simulation challenges students to apply their knowledge of business fundamentals in a practical setting.

Skill Development: This scenario enhances skills in strategic planning, market analysis, and entrepreneurial thinking.

Managing a Budget:

In budget management simulations, students must allocate limited resources effectively to cover operational costs, marketing, employee salaries, and other expenses. They learn to make financial decisions that will impact the health of the business.

Skill Development: This teaches financial literacy, critical decision-making, and prioritization—skills essential for any business leader.

Developing a Marketing Plan:

Students develop comprehensive marketing strategies based on real or hypothetical products or services. They need to consider several marketing channels, consumer psychology, and competitive positioning.

Skill Development: This simulation enhances understanding of market dynamics, promotional strategies, and consumer engagement techniques.

Benefits of Simulations in PBL:

Simulations provide a dynamic learning environment where students can experiment with business decisions and see the consequences of their actions in a risk-free setting. This experiential learning helps students better understand the complexities of running a business and prepares them for real-world challenges.

Research Support:

Studies have shown that simulations in business education significantly enhance student engagement and learning outcomes. According to Bellotti et al. (2013), using serious games and simulations in entrepreneurship education can lead to higher retention rates and a better understanding of complex business concepts. Another study by Faria et al. (2009) emphasizes that simulations provide an effective way for students to apply theoretical knowledge in practical, real-world scenarios, thereby enhancing their problem-solving and decision-making skills.

Critical Thinking and Problem Solving through Project-Based Learning

Project-based learning (PBL) is an educational approach that plays a crucial role in developing critical thinking and problem-solving skills. By engaging students in real-world challenges and encouraging them to devise and implement solutions, PBL fosters an environment where critical thinking and creativity are paramount.

Enhancing Critical Thinking and Problem Solving

Process of Problem Identification:

Understanding the Problem: In PBL, the first step involves students identifying and understanding the complexities of a problem. This requires them to gather information, ask pertinent questions, and analyze the situation comprehensively.

Skill Development: This stage enhances students' analytical skills, enabling them to dissect problems effectively and recognize underlying issues that need addressing.

Brainstorming Solutions:

- **Creative Ideation:** Once the problem is clearly defined, students brainstorm multiple solutions, encouraging creative and divergent thinking. This stage allows for the exploration of innovative ideas without the constraint of immediate feasibility.
- **Skill Development:** Brainstorming strengthens creative thinking skills and promotes an open-minded approach to problem-solving, crucial for entrepreneurial success.

Testing Hypotheses:

- **Experimentation:** Students select promising solutions and develop prototypes or plans to test their ideas. This experimental phase is critical for applying theoretical knowledge to practical scenarios.
- **Skill Development:** By testing their hypotheses, students learn to implement and adapt their ideas based on real-world constraints, improving their pragmatic problem-solving skills.

Iterating Based on Feedback:

- **Feedback Integration:** Critical feedback is solicited from peers, instructors, or industry professionals, providing external perspectives on the viability and effectiveness of the solutions.
- **Skill Development:** Learning to iterate based on feedback fosters resilience and adaptability, skills that are invaluable in constantly changing business environments.

Benefits of PBL in Developing These Skills

Project-based learning does not just teach students to solve problems but also to think critically about the steps they take and the solutions they develop. This reflective aspect of PBL is crucial for deep learning and lasting skill development.

Research Support:

Research has demonstrated the effectiveness of PBL in enhancing critical thinking and problem-solving skills. According to a study by Bell (2010), students engaged in PBL exhibited significantly improved problem-solving abilities and were better able to apply these skills in unfamiliar contexts. Another study by Wurdinger and Carlson (2010) supports the idea that PBL not only improves critical thinking but also prepares students for real-life challenges by simulating real-world tasks.

Collaborative Projects in Entrepreneurship Education

Collaborative projects are a cornerstone of entrepreneurship education, enabling students to work in teams to solve real-world business problems. This approach not only enhances business acumen but also fosters the development of essential teamwork and communication skills. Here, we explore how collaborative projects can be structured and highlight their impact on student learning through specific examples.

Examples of Collaborative Projects

Startup Launch Project:

Description: Students form teams to create a startup from the ground up. This includes market research, product development, business plan creation, and pitching to potential investors. Each team member assumes a role that plays to their strengths, whether in marketing, finance, operations, or product design.

Learning Outcomes: Students learn to integrate various business functions, collaborate under pressure, and communicate their ideas persuasively. They also gain firsthand experience in handling the uncertainties and challenges of launching a startup.

Social Enterprise Challenge:

- **Description:** Teams are tasked with developing a business model that addresses a social or environmental issue. The project involves researching the problem, engaging with the community to understand the impact, and designing a business solution that is both sustainable and profitable.
- **Learning Outcomes:** This project emphasizes ethical decision-making, social responsibility, and the ability to design business solutions that make a positive impact on society. Students learn the value of stakeholder engagement and the importance of building community trust.

International Business Strategy Competition:

Description: Student teams compete by developing business strategies for companies looking to enter or expand in international markets. This involves analyzing global market trends, understanding cultural differences, and proposing entry strategies that minimize risk and maximize potential.

Learning Outcomes: Students enhance their global business understanding, improve their strategic thinking skills, and learn how to communicate complex ideas effectively across diverse teams.

Benefits of Collaborative Projects

Teamwork Development:
Collaborative projects encourage students to work together, pooling their diverse skills and perspectives to achieve a common goal. This experience is invaluable in teaching the dynamics of effective team management and conflict resolution.

Communication Skills:

As students work together and present their projects to peers and evaluators, they refine their communication skills, learning to argue their points clearly and respond to feedback constructively.

Research Support:
Studies have shown that collaborative projects significantly enhance both the soft skills and business competencies of students. According to Laal and Ghodsi (2012), teamwork and collaborative learning can greatly improve problem-solving abilities and increase engagement and motivation among students. Another study by Michaelsen and Sweet (2008) highlights that well-designed team projects can lead to deeper learning and better retention of business concepts.

Social Entrepreneurship

Projects with Purpose: Solving Societal Issues

Social entrepreneurship stands at the intersection of business acumen and social innovation, focusing on developing business ideas that directly address societal challenges. In entrepreneurship education, a significant emphasis is placed on encouraging students to create ventures that contribute positively to society, tackling issues such as environmental sustainability, education, healthcare, and poverty reduction.

Conceptual Framework

Integration into Curriculum:
Social entrepreneurship is integrated into the curriculum through projects that require students to identify a social issue and then develop a business model to address it. This process includes market research, identification of community needs,

and the creation of a sustainable business plan that achieves social impact alongside financial viability.

Examples of Student Projects:

Environmental Sustainability: Students might develop a business that helps reduce waste through innovative recycling processes or by creating products from recycled materials.

Education: Projects could focus on educational technologies or programs that enhance access to quality education in underserved communities.

Healthcare: Student ventures might aim to improve healthcare delivery through mobile health solutions or affordable medical technologies.

Poverty Reduction: Projects could include the development of microfinance institutions aimed at entrepreneurs in low-income regions or businesses that provide affordable, essential goods and services to underprivileged populations.

Learning Outcomes

Cultivating Social Responsibility:
By working on these projects, students develop a strong sense of social responsibility. They learn how businesses can be a force for good, creating value that extends beyond profit to include social benefits.

Innovation for Social Good:

Students are taught to think creatively about how to use business tools to solve social problems. This often involves innovation in product design, service delivery, and business models.

Research Support

Evidence of Impact:
Research indicates that engaging in social entrepreneurship projects enhances students' empathy towards social issues and increases their motivation to engage in social change. According to a study by Tracey and Phillips (2007), social entrepreneurship education can significantly influence students' attitudes and career trajectories, orienting them more towards social impact.

Community Engagement:

Projects often involve direct interaction with community members, which enhances the learning experience by providing real-world feedback and increasing the relevance and impact of the academic work.

Community Engagement in Social Entrepreneurship Projects

Community engagement is a fundamental aspect of social entrepreneurship projects, playing a critical role in their success and sustainability. By involving community stakeholders directly in these projects, students not only enhance their learning experience but also gain invaluable insights into the specific needs and dynamics of the communities they aim to serve.

Involving Community Stakeholders

Direct Interaction:
Social entrepreneurship projects often begin with direct interaction with community members to identify and understand local challenges. This engagement may take the form of interviews, surveys, or community meetings, which provide students with a deeper understanding of the problems from the perspective of those most affected.

Co-creation of Solutions:
Community members are not just informants but active participants in creating solutions. This collaborative approach ensures that the solutions are culturally appropriate and directly address the community's needs. It also fosters a sense of ownership among community members, which is crucial for the project's long-term success.

Continuous Feedback:
Engaging with the community provides a continuous feedback loop that allows students to refine and adjust their projects based on real-world responses. This iterative process is essential for developing effective and sustainable business models.

Educational Benefits

Enhanced Learning Experience:
Real-world interaction with communities enriches the educational experience by providing students with practical insights into the complexities of social issues. This exposure helps

students apply theoretical knowledge in practical settings, enhancing their learning and retention.

Development of Empathy and Cultural Sensitivity:

Working closely with diverse social groups helps students develop greater empathy and cultural sensitivity. These skills are invaluable not only in social entrepreneurship but in any professional and personal interactions in an increasingly globalized world.

Research Support

Impact on Student Outcomes:

Research has shown that community engagement in educational projects can significantly enhance student outcomes. According to Astin and Sax (1998), students who participate in community service as part of their curriculum exhibit improved academic performance, increased interpersonal skills, and a higher level of civic responsibility.

Sustainability of Projects:

Community involvement also increases the sustainability of social ventures. A study by Bringle and Hatcher (2002) suggests that projects designed and implemented with community input are more likely to be sustainable over the long term because they are more aligned with the community's needs and resources.

Global Perspective in Social Entrepreneurship Education

Social entrepreneurship education not only addresses local community needs but also prepares students to tackle global challenges. By encouraging a global perspective, this educational approach equips students with the ability to develop solutions that are scalable and adaptable across different cultural contexts. This section explores how social entrepreneurship education fosters a broader understanding of global issues and cultivates the skills necessary for creating impactful, worldwide solutions.

Teaching a Global Perspective

Understanding Global Challenges:
Social entrepreneurship education begins with a comprehensive overview of global challenges such as poverty, climate change, and inequality. Students learn about these issues through case studies, current events, and discussions with experts and activists from around the world. This global focus helps students recognize the interconnectedness of these issues across different regions.

Scalable Solutions:

Students are taught to think beyond local solutions and consider how their ideas could be scaled globally. This involves studying successful international social enterprises and analyzing the factors that allowed these ventures to expand their impact across different geographical areas. Learning modules might focus on scalability strategies, such as franchising models, digital platforms, and partnerships with global organizations.

Cultural Adaptation:
An essential component of global perspective is understanding how to adapt solutions to fit different cultural contexts. Students engage in exercises that challenge them to modify their business models to respect cultural differences in areas such as communication styles, social norms, and economic conditions. These activities emphasize the importance of cultural sensitivity and customization in international expansion.

Research Support

Enhanced Global Understanding:
Research indicates that social entrepreneurship education can significantly enhance students' understanding of global issues. A study by Mair and Marti (2006) highlights that exposure to social entrepreneurship concepts increases students' awareness of societal problems and motivates them to think internationally about solutions.

Developing Global Leaders:

Social entrepreneurship education is effective in developing global leaders who are adept at navigating cross-cultural challenges. According to Hart and Milstein (2003), this educational approach cultivates a generation of leaders who are proactive, culturally aware, and committed to sustainable development worldwide.

Conclusion and Future Outlook: Preparing Future Leaders

As we reflect on the transformative impact of entrepreneurship education, it becomes evident that this form of learning is not merely about cultivating business acumen—it is about shaping future leaders who are equipped to navigate and influence a complex world. This chapter has explored the multifaceted benefits of entrepreneurship education, highlighting how it prepares students for leadership roles by instilling a unique blend of skills that are critical for both personal success and societal advancement.

Summarizing Key Learnings

Business Savvy:

Entrepreneurship education equips students with essential business skills, including strategic planning, financial management, and market analysis. These skills are fundamental for anyone looking to lead a venture, whether it's a startup or a multinational corporation. By engaging in real-world business scenarios and simulations, students not only learn the theoretical underpinnings of business operations but also apply these concepts in practical settings, preparing them for the challenges of the business world.

Ethical Grounding:

A core component of entrepreneurship education is its focus on ethics and social responsibility. Students learn to consider the wider impact of business decisions on society and the environment, fostering a sense of moral responsibility. This ethical grounding is crucial as businesses increasingly need to balance profitability with social and environmental sustainability to achieve long-term success.

Proactive Problem-Solving:

Through project-based learning and collaborative projects, students develop advanced problem-solving skills. They learn to think critically, address complex challenges, and innovate under pressure. These skills are essential for leadership as they enable individuals to navigate obstacles effectively and turn challenges into opportunities.

Reinforcing the Importance of These Skills

The skills developed through entrepreneurship education are not only valuable; they are essential for the next generation of leaders. In today's globalized and rapidly changing environment, leaders need more than just technical knowledge; they need the ability to think broadly, act ethically, and innovate continuously. Entrepreneurship education fosters these competencies, preparing students to:

Drive Innovation: By encouraging creativity and a can-do attitude, entrepreneurship education prepares students to be at the forefront of innovation, driving new technologies, services, and products that can transform industries.

Enhance Societal Well-being: With a strong emphasis on social entrepreneurship, students are motivated to apply their skills and resources to solve pressing societal problems, contributing to a healthier, more equitable society.

Adapt to Global Changes: The global perspective integrated into entrepreneurship education ensures that students are prepared to work and lead in an international environment, understanding and embracing cultural and economic diversities.

Looking Ahead: The Future of Entrepreneurship Education

The future of entrepreneurship education looks promising, with increasing recognition of its value in fostering a holistic educational experience. As this field evolves, it will likely incorporate more advanced technologies, such as artificial intelligence and virtual reality, to further enhance learning and simulate complex business environments. Moreover, as the world faces new challenges, such as climate change and global health crises, the next wave of entrepreneurship education will need to focus even more on developing leaders who are ready to tackle these issues head-on.

In conclusion, entrepreneurship education is a powerful tool for preparing future leaders who are innovative, ethical, and globally aware. By continuing to expand and evolve this educational framework, we can ensure that our future leaders are not only successful in their careers but also committed to making a positive impact on the world.

~ 5 ~

EXPERIENTIAL LEARNING MODELS

Case-Based Learning

Implementation of Case-Based Learning

Case-based learning (CBL) is a dynamic instructional strategy that uses detailed case studies to teach students about practical business and economic principles. This method engages students by placing them in the role of decision-makers, confronting them with real-life challenges that require complex problem-solving and strategic thinking.

Detailed Case Studies:

Scope and Diversity:

Global Business Scenarios: Educators utilize case studies from a wide array of businesses across the globe. These include everything from small entrepreneurial ventures in emerging markets to major multinational corporations facing global strategic issues. This diversity ensures that students gain exposure to varied business environments and challenges.

Economic Principles and Business Operations: Each case study provides practical insights into fundamental business concepts such as market analysis, operational strategy, financial forecasting, and ethical decision-making. For example, a case might explore how a tech startup in Silicon Valley scales operations internationally or how a major retailer adjusts its strategies in response to global economic downturns.

Pedagogical Benefits:

Application of Theory to Practice: By analyzing real-world scenarios, students can bridge the gap between theoretical economic principles and practical business applications. This not only reinforces learning but also enhances their analytical and critical thinking skills.

Enhanced Decision-Making: Students must weigh various strategic options and make decisions that mimic the complexities faced by actual businesses. This process improves their ability to think strategically and make informed decisions based on a mixture of analytical deduction and intuitive judgment.

Interactive Learning Environment:

Group Discussions and Debates: Case studies often form the basis for group discussions, presentations, and debates, fostering an interactive learning environment. This collaboration encourages students to articulate their thoughts, defend their positions, and critically evaluate the viewpoints of their peers.

Problem-Solving Workshops: Some programs include workshops where students role-play as business leaders to solve the issues presented in the cases. This active participation deepens their engagement and understanding of the material.

Research Support:

Studies have shown that case-based learning significantly enhances students' retention of material and their ability to apply knowledge to new situations. According to a study by Herreid (2007), students who engage in CBL exhibit a deeper understanding of subject matter and improved critical thinking skills. Furthermore, Yin (2014) highlights that CBL helps in developing managerial and leadership skills, as it simulates real-life leadership challenges.

Learning Outcomes of Case-Based Learning

Case-Based Learning (CBL) through offering students a unique opportunity to dive deep into the complexities of real-world business scenarios. This method is particularly effective in enhancing students' understanding of nuanced decision-making, economic forecasting, and strategic planning across diverse cultural and economic contexts.

Enhancing Decision-Making Skills

Complex Problem Solving:
CBL forces students to confront complex business problems that do not have straightforward solutions. Through analysis of detailed case studies, students learn to assess various factors

and potential outcomes before making decisions. This practice develops their ability to think critically and make well-informed decisions under pressure.

Contextual Decision-Making:
Real-world cases provide a context that textbooks cannot, offering students insights into how decisions are influenced by real-world constraints and pressures. This includes understanding how cultural, economic, and competitive environments impact strategic choices.

Mastery of Economic Forecasting

Analytical Application:
Case studies often involve scenarios that require students to engage in economic forecasting to predict future market trends and business performance. This involves interpreting economic data, considering market dynamics, and applying statistical tools to make educated predictions.

Practical Relevance:
Students learn to connect theoretical economic models with practical business applications. For example, analyzing a case study about a startup might involve forecasting demand for a new product in different economic conditions, teaching students how external economic factors influence business growth.

Strategic Planning in Diverse Contexts

Global Perspective:
Many case studies used in CBL are set in a variety of international contexts, exposing students to global business strategies and challenges. This helps students learn how to plan and execute business strategies in a way that is sensitive to cultural and economic differences across regions.

Long-term Strategic Thinking:
CBL helps students understand the importance of strategic planning in ensuring long-term business success. Through cases, students explore how businesses develop and implement strategies to achieve sustainable competitive advantages.

Research Support

Educational Impact:
According to research by Khatri et al. (2018), CBL significantly improves students' problem-solving abilities, their capacity for critical thinking, and their overall academic performance. The study emphasizes that case-based learning not only deepens theoretical understanding but also enhances the ability to apply knowledge in practical situations.

Integration into Curriculum: Case-Based Learning

Integrating case-based learning into the business education curriculum involves strategic planning to ensure that students not only absorb the content but also actively engage with it to develop critical thinking, communication, and decision-making skills. This section outlines effective classroom strategies for discussing case studies and details assessment techniques that measure the depth of students' learning.

Discussion and Analysis

Classroom Strategies:

Group Discussions: One of the primary strategies for discussing case studies is through structured group discussions. In these sessions, students are divided into small groups to analyze specific aspects of a case study. This encourages collaboration and allows students to pool their collective knowledge and perspectives. The group setting also helps shy students become more engaged when they see the participation of their peers.

Written Analyses: Students are often required to submit written analyses of case studies. These assignments prompt students to not only summarize the case but also critically evaluate the decisions made by the business and suggest alternative strategies. This written component helps develop their formal communication skills and ability to articulate complex ideas clearly and concisely.

Role-Playing Exercises: Role-playing is an engaging way to bring case studies to life. Students assume the roles of different stakeholders in a business scenario—such as a company's executive team, employees, customers, or suppliers—and act out the decision-making process. This method helps students understand the diverse perspectives involved in business situations and the complexities of balancing competing interests.

Assessment Techniques

Measuring Analytical Skills and Practical Application:

Case Study Reports: Students can be assessed through detailed reports where they analyze the case study, recommend solutions, and justify their choices based on theoretical knowledge. These reports provide a comprehensive view of the student's ability to integrate and apply learning effectively.

Presentations: Oral presentations of case study analyses are an excellent way for students to demonstrate their understanding. Presentations often involve defending their solutions to an audience, which could include peers, instructors, or even external business experts. This format tests their ability to clearly and persuasively communicate their ideas.

Peer Review: Incorporating peer review in the assessment process can provide valuable insights into how students perceive and evaluate each other's understanding and application of case study material. This not only helps students learn to assess critical business situations but also encourages a deeper engagement with the content as they prepare to critique their peers' work.

Evaluating Understanding of Economic and Societal Implications:

Reflective Essays: After working through a case study, students can be tasked with writing a reflective essay that explores the broader economic, social, and ethical implications of the business decisions discussed. This assessment technique encourages students to connect classroom knowledge with real-world business practices and societal impacts.

Scenario Analysis: Students may be given hypothetical follow-up scenarios to the original case study and asked to predict outcomes based on different business decisions. This helps gauge their understanding of cause and effect in complex business environments.

By carefully integrating discussion and analysis strategies into the curriculum and employing multifaceted assessment techniques, educators can significantly enhance the effectiveness of case-based learning. These methods ensure that students not only grasp the theoretical underpinnings of business practices but also appreciate the practical implications of business decisions in a real-world context. This holistic approach to learning prepares students for the challenges of the business world, equipping them with the necessary skills to succeed and lead.

Interactive Projects

Project Design and Implementation

Interactive projects form a core part of experiential learning models in entrepreneurship education, emphasizing student involvement and practical outcomes. These projects are carefully designed to mirror real-world business challenges, requiring active participation and resulting in tangible outcomes that have direct implications for actual businesses or organizations.

Real-World Business Projects:

Scope and Objectives:

Projects are tailored to solve specific business problems or exploit opportunities within various market contexts. This requires students to engage deeply with the problem and understand the business's environment, market, and internal capabilities.

Examples might include developing a comprehensive marketing strategy for a local startup, designing a product tailored to the needs of an underserved market, or optimizing the supply chain processes for a nonprofit organization to enhance operational efficiency.

Collaborative Design:

Students typically work in teams to foster a collaborative learning environment. This teamwork mimics real business settings where cross-functional teams work together to solve complex problems.

Educators often partner with real businesses or community organizations to provide students with authentic challenges. This partnership allows students to work on projects that have genuine business implications, enhancing the learning experience and providing real value to external stakeholders.

Application of Theoretical Knowledge:

Students apply concepts learned in classes—such as market analysis, business strategy, operational management, and financial planning—to their projects. This application helps bridge the gap between theoretical knowledge and practical implementation.

Technology Integration:

Modern technology tools are often integrated into these projects to analyze data, enhance designs, or improve communication and project management. For instance, students might use CRM software to manage customer relationships for a marketing project or CAD tools for product design.

Research Support:

Educational Outcomes:
Research by Bell (2010) highlights that project-based learning, especially when integrated with real-world business challenges, significantly enhances problem-solving skills, creativity, and engagement among students.

According to Kolb and Kolb (2005), these types of interactive projects also foster deeper learning and retention because they involve active experimentation and reflective observation, key components of experiential learning.

Collaboration and Impact in Interactive Projects

Interactive projects within entrepreneurship education are characterized by their collaborative nature, which not only enhances the learning experience but also mimics the team-based work environment of the business world. This section highlights the importance of collaboration in these projects and discusses how it impacts both the students and the community or business partners involved.

The Importance of Team-Based Work

Fostering Teamwork:
Interactive projects require students to work in teams, where each member often brings a unique skill set and perspective. This diversity promotes a comprehensive approach to problem-solving and decision-making. Teams are tasked with coordinating their efforts, managing project timelines, and achieving shared goals, which mirrors the collaborative nature of modern workplaces.

Communication Skills:

Effective communication is crucial in these projects, as students must articulate ideas, negotiate roles, and resolve conflicts. They also need to maintain clear and ongoing communication with external stakeholders, which can include community leaders, business owners, or nonprofit organizations, depending on the project's focus.

Project Management:

Students are responsible for managing the entire lifecycle of the project, from initial planning and design to implementation and final delivery. This process involves setting clear objectives, scheduling tasks, monitoring progress, and adjusting plans as necessary to meet deadlines and deliverables.

Impact on Students and Partners

Real Business Outcomes:

The results of these projects often have direct implications for the business or community partners. For instance, a student-developed marketing plan might be implemented by a local business, directly affecting its market reach and profitability. Similarly, a strategy to improve operational efficiencies could significantly reduce costs for a nonprofit organization.

Community Engagement and Social Impact:

Many projects are designed with a community focus, where the primary goal is to achieve a social impact. This could involve developing solutions to enhance local services, improve environmental sustainability, or boost economic development. The success of these projects can lead to long-term benefits for the community and enhance the relationship between the institution and the local area.

Research Support

Enhanced Learning and Professional Preparation:

According to research by Michaelsen and Sweet (2008), team-based projects significantly enhance students' problem-solving and interpersonal skills, better preparing them for their professional careers. These projects also improve students' abilities to handle real-world pressures and complexities.

Community and Organizational Benefits:

A study by Bringle and Hatcher (2002) demonstrates that community-based projects can lead to significant positive impacts on local organizations and populations, providing tangible benefits and strengthening community ties.

Skills Development in Interactive Projects

Interactive projects within entrepreneurship education serve as critical platforms for students to develop essential professional skills. Two pivotal areas of skill development through these projects are project management and innovation. This section explores how engaging in real-world projects enhances these competencies, which are vital for both personal and professional success.

Project Management Skills

Leadership and Team Coordination:
Managing real-world projects allows students to step into leadership roles within their teams, providing opportunities to coordinate efforts, mediate conflicts, and motivate peers. This hands-on experience helps them understand the dynamics of effective leadership and team management.

Project Planning and Execution:
Students learn to outline clear project objectives, plan various phases of the project lifecycle, allocate resources efficiently, and execute plans to achieve desired outcomes. They gain experience in using project management tools and methodologies, which are essential for keeping projects on track.

Resource Allocation and Deadline Management:
Real-world projects require students to work within the constraints of limited resources, including time, money, and manpower. Learning to allocate these resources wisely, while adhering to strict deadlines, teaches students critical skills in prioritization and time management.

Research Support:
A study by Turner and Müller (2004) highlights that engaging in project management tasks significantly enhances students' leadership and organizational skills, which are crucial for career advancement in any field.

Innovation and Creativity

Fostering Creativity in Problem-Solving:
Interactive projects challenge students to address complex, often ambiguous problems that lack straightforward solutions. This environment pushes them to think creatively, exploring innovative solutions that defy conventional approaches.

Design Thinking and Innovation:
Students are encouraged to employ design thinking processes, which focus on user-centric, prototype-driven solutions for complex problems. This approach fosters a mindset of innovation, emphasizing iterative testing and refinement of ideas.

Critical Implementation of Creative Ideas:
Beyond generating ideas, students must critically evaluate the feasibility and potential impact of their innovations. This involves assessing risks, predicting potential outcomes, and making adjustments to their proposals based on constructive feedback.

Research Support:
According to a study by Klimova and Poulova (2016), projects that require creative solutions enhance students' ability to innovate and adapt to new challenges, skills that are highly valued in today's dynamic job market.

Internships and Apprenticeships

Hands-on Experience

Internships and apprenticeships are crucial components of experiential learning models, bridging the gap between academic theories and real-world application. By partnering with businesses across various sectors, educational institutions offer students invaluable hands-on experiences that significantly enhance their learning and career readiness.

Partnerships with Businesses

Forming Collaborations:
Educational institutions actively collaborate with a diverse range of businesses, from local startups to major international corporations, to secure internships and apprenticeships. These partnerships are designed to be mutually beneficial, with businesses gaining access to emerging talent and students receiving practical experience.

Types of Internships and Apprenticeships:

Summer Internships: Typically lasting from one to three months, these internships allow students to work full-time on specific projects or within certain departments, providing a concentrated period of learning and professional development.

Co-operative Education (Co-op) Programs: These programs integrate academic studies with work experience in related fields. Students alternate between periods of study and work, which may last up to a year, gaining deeper industry insights and skills.

Part-time Internships: Often conducted during the academic year, part-time internships require students to balance their coursework with work responsibilities, offering a continuous work experience that complements their studies.

Apprenticeships: More common in technical and trades disciplines, apprenticeships involve a combination of on-the-job training and classroom instruction, allowing students to gain certified skills and sometimes a trade license.

Implementation and Integration into Curriculum

Curriculum Integration:

Many educational programs are designed to integrate internships and apprenticeships seamlessly into the curriculum. This integration ensures that the work experience is not just an adjunct to education but a core part of the learning process, often with specific academic credits assigned to these experiences.

Learning Objectives and Outcomes:

Each internship or apprenticeship is structured around clear learning objectives, which align with the student's academic and career goals. Regular assessments and feedback sessions help students reflect on their experiences and apply their on-site learning to their academic studies.

Research Support

Impact on Career Readiness:

Research indicates that students who participate in internships and apprenticeships show significantly higher levels of career readiness and report greater satisfaction with their post-graduate employment outcomes. A study by Knouse and Fontenot (2008) highlights that these experiences are critical in helping students transition smoothly into the workforce, enhancing their employability and job performance.

Skill Application and Development in K-12 Internships and Apprenticeships

Internships and apprenticeships are not only beneficial in higher education and vocational training but also offer significant advantages when integrated into K-12 education. These programs enable younger students to apply classroom knowledge in professional settings, which enhances their understanding of industry practices and sets a foundation for future learning and career choices.

Application of Classroom Knowledge

Real-World Context:
K-12 internships and apprenticeships provide students with the opportunity to see how their classroom learning applies to real-world situations. For instance, math skills can be applied in accounting tasks, science knowledge can be utilized in laboratory settings, and language arts skills can be employed in communication and documentation tasks.

Enhancement of Academic Concepts:

By participating in these experiences, students can see the practical implications of their studies, which often leads to a deeper understanding and appreciation of the material. This relevance can increase motivation and engagement back in the classroom, as students understand the practical benefits of their education.

Development of Professional Skills

Introduction to Industry Practices:

Even brief exposures to professional environments allow students to observe and understand workplace norms and industry practices. These experiences demystify the world of work, making it more accessible and less intimidating for young learners.

Expectation Setting:

Engaging with professionals and performing real work tasks helps students learn about the expectations in various fields. This early exposure is invaluable as it can influence their future educational and career paths by providing insights into what various jobs entail and the skills they require.

Integration in School Curriculum

Structured Learning:

Schools often structure these programs to align with educational standards and learning outcomes. This structured approach ensures that the internships and apprenticeships are not just additional activities but integral parts of the educational process, designed to complement and enhance the traditional curriculum.

Mentorship and Guidance:

Professional mentors in these programs play a crucial role. They guide students, provide feedback, and help them connect their school-based learning with real-world applications. This mentorship enriches the learning experience and provides students with a model of professional behavior.

Research Support

Impact on Learning and Career Orientation:

Research by Christensen and Knezek (2017) demonstrates that early work-based learning experiences can significantly impact students' academic performance and career interests. These experiences are shown to enhance problem-solving skills, increase engagement, and influence career aspirations positively.

Benefits to Students and Companies

Internships and apprenticeships are transformative components of experiential learning, offering substantial benefits not only to the students who participate in them but also to the companies that host these aspiring professionals. These programs are instrumental in enhancing career readiness and providing invaluable on-the-job feedback that shapes students' future careers.

Career Readiness

Enhanced Employability:

Internships and apprenticeships equip students with a set of demonstrable skills that are highly valued in the workforce. By participating in these programs, students gain practical experience that complements their academic knowledge, making them more attractive to future employers.

These experiences also allow students to build a professional network, connecting with individuals who can provide career advice, recommendations, and job opportunities. This network is often crucial for securing employment after graduation.

Portfolio Development:
During their internships or apprenticeships, students work on real projects that contribute to their portfolios. This portfolio of work can significantly enhance a student's resume, providing tangible evidence of their skills and abilities to prospective employers.

The diversity of tasks and responsibilities handled during these placements also demonstrates the student's ability to adapt to various roles and challenges, further bolstering their employability.

Feedback and Evaluation

Role of Continuous Feedback:
One of the key benefits of internships and apprenticeships is the ongoing feedback provided by supervisors and mentors. This feedback is vital for students' professional development as it helps them identify strengths and areas for improvement.

Regular evaluations allow students to refine their skills continually and adjust their learning strategies throughout their placement, enhancing their overall business acumen and professional demeanor.

Mentorship Impact:

Mentors play a significant role in shaping the students' experience. They offer guidance, share insights from their own career paths, and provide support, which can significantly influence a student's professional growth and confidence.

Research Support

Empirical Evidence:

Research by Narayanan, Olk, and Fukami (2010) found that internships significantly improve students' readiness for the workforce by providing them with real-world experience and networking opportunities that are not typically available through classroom learning alone.

Additionally, a study by Gault, Redington, and Schlager (2000) highlights that students who participate in internships receive higher job offers and report greater job satisfaction, underscoring the direct benefits of these experiences on career outcomes.

Conclusion and Future Directions

Synthesis of Experiential Learning Benefits

Experiential learning models have shown a profound impact on the educational and professional trajectories of K-12 students. By merging theoretical knowledge with practical application, these models not only enhance learning outcomes but also prepare students for real-world challenges and opportunities. The integration of case-based learning, interactive projects, and internships and apprenticeships into the K-12 curriculum transforms traditional education, making it more dynamic and relevant.

Transformative Impact:

Experiential learning enables students to apply classroom theories in real-world scenarios, which solidifies their understanding and retention of knowledge. For instance, through case-based learning, students tackle complex business issues, enhancing their analytical and decision-making skills. Interactive projects foster creativity and innovation, while internships and apprenticeships provide a platform for students to develop professional skills and build networks that are crucial for their future careers.

Blending Knowledge and Practice:

This educational approach ensures that students are not just passive recipients of information but active participants in their learning journey. They learn to solve problems, think critically, and communicate effectively—skills that are vital in any career path they choose to follow.

Investment in Experiential Learning:

Investment should not only be financial but also involve a commitment to developing quality programs that meet the diverse needs of students. This includes training teachers, forming partnerships with businesses, and continually assessing and improving experiential learning initiatives.

Highlighting Proven Benefits:

The evidence supporting the effectiveness of experiential learning in preparing students for successful careers is compelling. Studies have consistently shown that students who engage in experiential learning are better equipped for the workforce and more adaptable to changing industries and new technologies.

Future Directions:

Looking forward, the focus should be on scaling these programs to reach a broader range of students and incorporating technology to enhance and extend the reach of experiential learning. There is also a growing need to tailor experiential learning programs to address the emerging demands of the global economy.

As we move into a future where education increasingly intersects with innovation and practical application, experiential learning stands as a crucial element of student development. It is imperative that all educational stakeholders work collaboratively to expand these opportunities, ensuring that every student has the chance to benefit from an education that is as comprehensive as it is transformative. The call to action is clear: invest in, support, and expand experiential learning to equip the next generation with the skills, knowledge, and experience they need to succeed in the ever-evolving professional landscape.

IMPLEMENTING STEAMPRENEURSHIP IN SCHOOLS

Curriculum Design

Step-by-Step Integration Guide

Integrating Steampreneurship into existing school curricula requires a strategic and methodical approach. This section provides a detailed guide on how to effectively incorporate Steampreneurship elements into the curriculum, ensuring a seamless blend of traditional and innovative educational models.

Assessment of Current Curriculum

Initial Evaluation:
Identify Core Learning Objectives: The first step in integrating Steampreneurship is to conduct a comprehensive review

of the existing curriculum across all subjects to understand the core learning objectives currently in place. This understanding allows for the identification of natural intersections where Steampreneurship methodologies can enhance or complement the learning outcomes.

Gap Analysis:

Spot Opportunities for Integration: Look for areas within the current curriculum that could benefit from real-world applications, such as projects or case studies that align with Steampreneurship principles. This might include adding entrepreneurial projects in economics classes, integrating real-world problem-solving into science courses, or incorporating social entrepreneurship concepts into social studies.

Stakeholder Engagement:

Consultation with Educators and Administrators: Engaging with teachers, curriculum designers, and school administrators is crucial during the assessment phase. Their insights can help pinpoint practical and logistical considerations and foster a collaborative approach to curriculum redesign.

Feedback from Students: Gathering input from students can provide valuable perspectives on which areas of their education could be more engaging or applicable to real-life scenarios.

Research Support

Evidence-Based Integration:

Review of Educational Research: Drawing on existing research about the benefits of experiential learning can guide the integration process. Studies have shown that experiential learning approaches, such as those used in Steampreneurship, can significantly enhance student engagement, understanding, and retention of material.

Incorporation of Steampreneurship Elements

Integrating Steampreneurship into the curriculum involves embedding Steampreneurship modules within existing subjects, enhancing the relevance and application of classroom learning to real-world contexts. This strategic placement of Steampreneurship elements fosters a deeper understanding of subject matter and cultivates a practical skill set in students.

Practical Strategies for Incorporation

Alignment with Current Subjects:

Economic Principles in Math Classes: Utilize economic models and financial calculations to teach mathematical concepts. For example, apply algebraic equations to solve problems related to interest rates, loan payments, or financial forecasting, which not only teaches math but also basic financial literacy.

Ethical Considerations in Science Projects: Integrate ethical discussions into science curricula by evaluating case studies that explore the implications of scientific advances, such as genetic engineering or environmental conservation. This approach encourages students to think critically about the impact of science on society and the environment.

Development of Entrepreneurial Mindset:

Entrepreneurial Projects in Social Studies: Embed projects that require students to develop business plans addressing social issues discussed in class. This could involve designing a business that helps alleviate local poverty or improves community health, linking social studies with real-world entrepreneurial initiatives.

Innovation in Technology Education: Encourage students to develop new products or services as part of their technology classes, fostering creativity and problem-solving skills.

Research Support

Educational Benefits of Steampreneurship Integration:

Research indicates that the integration of real-world applications into the curriculum significantly enhances student engagement and learning outcomes. A study by Bell (2010) found that students who engaged in applied learning activities, such as those promoted by Steampreneurship, were better able to understand complex concepts and more likely to retain information long-term.

Additionally, the integration of ethical considerations into science and technology education has been shown to increase students' awareness of the societal impacts of their work, promoting a more responsible approach to scientific inquiry and innovation.

Interdisciplinary Projects

Interdisciplinary projects are pivotal in implementing Steampreneurship within schools, as they encourage students to apply skills and knowledge from various disciplines to solve real-world problems. These projects blend academic learning with practical application, fostering entrepreneurial thinking and innovation.

Design and Implementation of Interdisciplinary Projects

Project Scope and Objectives:

Combining Disciplines: Projects are designed to require input from multiple academic subjects. For example, a project might combine principles of science (such as environmental science), technology (such as information technology), engineering (such as product design), arts (such as marketing and user experience), and mathematics (such as budgeting and statistics).

Real-World Applications: Each project is rooted in addressing a tangible problem or need, which could range from designing eco-friendly packaging to creating a business plan for a startup aimed at solving a local issue like food waste.

Entrepreneurial Focus:

Problem Identification and Solution Development: Students begin by identifying a real-world problem, then brainstorm potential solutions based on their interdisciplinary knowledge. This process encourages them to think like entrepreneurs, identifying market needs and devising practical solutions.

Prototype and Market Strategy: Students develop prototypes and outline a market entry strategy, considering the economic, environmental, and social impacts of their proposed solutions.

Research Support

Benefits of Interdisciplinary Learning:
Studies have shown that interdisciplinary projects enhance critical thinking, creativity, and problem-solving abilities. A report by Jacobs (1989) emphasizes that such projects help students integrate knowledge from different domains, which is crucial for innovation.

Further, interdisciplinary learning has been linked to increased motivation and engagement among students, as found in a study by Newell (1994), because it makes learning more relevant and applied.

Entrepreneurial Thinking in Education:

According to a study by Lackéus (2015), engaging students in entrepreneurial projects within educational settings significantly boosts their self-efficacy, motivation, and overall personal development. These projects prepare students not just academically but also emotionally and socially for future challenges.

Development of New Courses

Incorporating Steampreneurship into school curricula often necessitates the development of new courses specifically designed to address the unique aspects of entrepreneurship, innovation, and experiential learning. These courses are crucial for fostering a comprehensive understanding and application of Steampreneurship principles among students.

Specialized Steampreneurship Courses

Course Design:

Focus Areas: New courses can be designed to focus exclusively on various elements of entrepreneurship such as business model creation, startup finance, market analysis, and innovation management. These courses provide an in-depth understanding of entrepreneurial processes and decision-making.

Experiential Learning Components: Each course should include practical components such as project-based learning, case studies, and real-world problem-solving activities to enhance the experiential learning aspects.

Elective or Mandatory: Depending on the school's curriculum structure, these courses can be offered as electives to students who have a particular interest in entrepreneurship or as mandatory courses to ensure all students acquire basic entrepreneurial skills.

Collaboration Across Departments

Interdepartmental Cooperation:

Co-Design of Courses: Encourage collaboration between different academic departments (e.g., Business, Science, Technology, and Arts) to co-design courses that integrate knowledge and skills from multiple disciplines. This approach ensures that the courses are rich in content and diverse in perspective.

Co-Delivery of Courses: Implement co-teaching strategies where educators from different disciplines work together to deliver courses. This not only enriches the teaching process but also models collaborative, interdisciplinary thinking for students.

Research Support

Effectiveness of Specialized Courses:

Research by Fayolle and Gailly (2008) has shown that well-designed entrepreneurship education programs, including specialized courses, can significantly enhance students' entrepreneurial intentions and capabilities by providing targeted knowledge and skills.

Benefits of Interdisciplinary Education:

Technology Integration

Technology Integration

Integrating technology into the Steampreneurship curriculum enhances the learning experience by providing students with modern tools that support collaboration, project management, and real-time communication. The strategic use of digital platforms is essential in facilitating the dynamic and interactive nature of Steampreneurship projects.

Enhancing Learning with Technology

Digital Platforms:

Learning Management Systems (LMS): Platforms like Google Classroom and Moodle offer robust environments where educators can distribute materials, collect assignments, and facilitate discussions. These systems are crucial for organizing and managing coursework, especially in courses that involve a significant amount of collaborative project work.

Project Management Tools: Specialized software such as Asana, Trello, or Microsoft Project can be used to manage Steampreneurship projects effectively. These tools help students keep track of deadlines, assign tasks, and monitor progress, which are essential skills in entrepreneurship and project management.

Collaboration Software: Tools like Slack, Microsoft Teams, or Zoom facilitate real-time communication and collaboration among students, which is vital for team-based projects that simulate real-world business environments.

Research Support

Impact of Technology on Learning:

Facilitating Engagement and Collaboration: Research by Means et al. (2013) demonstrated that technology, particularly collaborative tools, enhances student engagement and fosters a more collaborative learning environment. These tools allow students to work together effectively, even from different locations, making it possible to undertake complex, interdisciplinary projects that mirror real-world business tasks.

Improving Project Management Skills: A study by Kapp and O'Driscoll (2010) highlights how project management tools can significantly improve students' abilities to plan, execute, and monitor project tasks, skills that are essential for successful entrepreneurship.

Technology Integration: Interactive Tools

In the realm of Steampreneurship, the utilization of advanced interactive tools such as simulation software, virtual reality (VR), and augmented reality (AR) plays a pivotal role in enhancing the educational experience. These technologies offer immersive experiences that simulate real-world challenges, allowing students to explore complex scenarios in a controlled yet dynamic environment.

Implementing Interactive Tools

Simulation Software:

Business Simulations: Tools like Capsim and Marketplace Simulations allow students to manage virtual businesses in competitive environments. These simulations challenge students to apply their knowledge of marketing, operations, and finance in real-time, reinforcing theoretical knowledge through practical application.

Virtual Reality (VR):

Immersive Learning Scenarios: VR can transport students into realistic, three-dimensional environments where they can interact with virtual elements as if they were in a real-world setting. For example, VR can simulate the experience of running a retail store or negotiating with suppliers, providing a deep, experiential understanding of business operations.

Enhanced Engagement: VR experiences are highly engaging, making complex concepts more accessible and memorable by providing a visual and interactive way to learn.

Augmented Reality (AR):

Overlaying Information: AR can superimpose information or visualizations on the real world, enhancing the learning experience. For instance, AR can be used to display data about consumer behavior or market trends during field trips to businesses or other relevant locations.

Practical Applications: In subjects like product design or architecture, AR can allow students to see their designs superimposed onto existing environments, providing immediate feedback on how their ideas would work in a real context.

Research Support

Enhancing Learning Outcomes:

Studies have shown that the use of VR and AR in education can significantly enhance student understanding and retention of information. According to a study by Fowler (2015), VR environments promote an active learning process that is more engaging and effective than traditional learning methods.

Similarly, AR has been found to improve the ability to apply knowledge in practical settings, as highlighted in research by Billinghurst and Duenser (2012), which shows that AR applications in educational settings enhance problem-solving skills and engagement.

Technology Training for Educators

As schools increasingly incorporate technology into their curricula through Steampreneurship, it is crucial to ensure that educators are equipped with the necessary skills to effectively use and integrate these technologies into their teaching. Effective technology training programs for educators not only enhance the learning experience for students but also empower teachers to confidently utilize modern educational tools.

Tech-Savvy Training Programs

Comprehensive Technology Training:
Basic IT Skills: Training programs should begin with foundational IT skills for educators who may need an introduction or a refresher course on basic computer skills, internet navigation, and common software tools.

Advanced Technology Integration: Beyond basic skills, educators require specialized training on how to integrate specific educational technologies into their teaching practices. This includes training on learning management systems (LMS) like Google Classroom or Moodle, as well as more sophisticated tools like simulation software, VR, and AR applications.

Customized Workshops and Seminars:

Workshop Sessions: Interactive workshops provide hands-on experiences with new technologies, allowing educators to explore and practice using these tools in a supportive environment.

Follow-Up Seminars: Seminars can offer deeper insights into the pedagogical implications of technology use in the classroom and discuss best practices for integrating these tools into various teaching strategies.

Research Support

Effectiveness of Educator Technology Training:

Research underscores the importance of comprehensive technology training for teachers. A study by Ertmer and Ottenbreit-Leftwich (2010) highlights that while teachers generally recognize the value of using technology in the classroom, their practical ability to integrate technology is significantly enhanced through targeted training programs.

Furthermore, Hew and Brush (2007) found that one of the major barriers to technology integration in education is the lack of adequate teacher training. Their study advocates for ongoing professional development in technology as a critical component for educational success.

Feedback and Evaluation Technologies

In the context of Steampreneurship, effective use of technology for feedback and evaluation is crucial for monitoring student progress, providing timely feedback, and personalizing learning experiences. By equipping educators with the right tools and techniques, schools can ensure that assessment becomes a continuous and integral part of the learning process, tailored to meet individual student needs.

Implementing Feedback and Evaluation Technologies

Assessment Tools:

Learning Management Systems (LMS): Platforms such as Canvas, Moodle, and Google Classroom offer built-in tools for tracking student progress, submitting assignments, and conducting quizzes and exams. These systems allow educators to collect data on student performance continuously and use this data to adjust instructional strategies.

Adaptive Learning Software: Technologies like DreamBox or Knewton provide adaptive learning experiences, where the difficulty of tasks is adjusted based on the learner's performance, ensuring that each student can progress at their own pace.

Feedback Mechanisms:

Real-Time Feedback Tools: Applications such as Socrative or Kahoot allow educators to conduct real-time assessments and provide instant feedback to students. This immediacy helps students understand their learning gaps and achievements quickly.

Audio and Video Feedback Tools: Tools like Screencast-O-Matic or VoiceThread enable teachers to provide personalized audio or video feedback on assignments and projects, which can be more detailed and engaging than traditional written comments.

Personalization of Learning:

Data Analytics: Advanced data analytics tools can help educators analyze performance trends and create personalized learning paths for students. This approach is especially beneficial in identifying students who may need additional support or challenge.

Individual Learning Plans: Using technology to develop and monitor Individual Learning Plans (ILPs) allows educators to set specific goals for each student and track their progress over time, adjusting teaching methods and resources as needed.

Research Support

Enhancing Educational Outcomes:

A study by Means et al. (2013) found that technology-enhanced formative assessment methods significantly improve student engagement and academic performance by providing timely and personalized feedback.

Research by Xie, Ke, and Sharma (2018) demonstrates that personalized learning environments supported by technology lead to higher student satisfaction and better learning outcomes, as they cater to the individual learning styles and paces of students.

Advocacy for Expansion

As we culminate our discussion on Steampreneurship, it's crucial to underscore the transformative impact this educational approach has on student engagement, learning outcomes, and career readiness. The integration of Steampreneurship into school curricula not only revitalizes the educational experience but also bridges the often-cited gap between theoretical knowledge and practical application. This conclusion seeks to summarize these benefits, advocate for the expansion of Steampreneurship, and explore future directions for its implementation.

Summarizing the Benefits of Steampreneurship

Enhanced Student Engagement: Steampreneurship inherently involves learning activities that are interactive, collaborative, and directly tied to real-world applications. This approach has proven effective in capturing students' interest and sustaining their engagement over traditional methods. Engaged students are more likely to attend classes, participate actively, and achieve higher levels of academic performance.

Improved Learning Outcomes: Through projects that require critical thinking, problem-solving, and cross-disciplinary skills, students involved in Steampreneurship programs gain a deeper understanding of the material. They learn not only to apply knowledge in practical settings but also to connect concepts across various fields, leading to a more comprehensive educational experience. This holistic learning fosters adaptability and innovation, skills that are crucial in today's ever-evolving job market.

Enhanced Career Readiness: Steampreneurship programs excel in preparing students for the workforce by providing them with real-world experience, technical skills, and the opportunity to develop soft skills such as communication, teamwork, and leadership. The experiential component of Steampreneurship ensures that students graduate with a robust portfolio of demonstrable skills and experiences, making them highly competitive candidates for employment.

Advocacy for Steampreneurship in Education Systems

Call to Action for Stakeholders: The success and expansion of Steampreneurship depend on the active support of educators, school administrators, and policymakers. It is imperative that these stakeholders recognize the value of experiential learning and advocate for the integration of Steampreneurship into educational curricula. Support can manifest in various forms, such as policy amendments to include experiential learning credits, increased funding for Steampreneurship programs, and professional development opportunities for educators to effectively deliver Steampreneurship content.

Highlighting Proven Benefits: The benefits of Steampreneurship are not merely anecdotal; they are supported by a growing body of research that attests to its effectiveness in improving educational outcomes and preparing students for successful careers. Advocating for Steampreneurship involves presenting this evidence to decision-makers in education, demonstrating the direct correlation between experiential learning and student achievement, and emphasizing the necessity of these programs in preparing students for a complex, rapidly changing world.

Future Directions: Scaling and Sustainability

Expanding Reach and Accessibility: To maximize the impact of Steampreneurship, strategies must be developed to scale these programs to reach a broader demographic of students. This involves creating adaptable Steampreneurship models that can be implemented in diverse educational settings, from urban to rural schools, ensuring that all students have access to the benefits of experiential learning.

Building Partnerships: Strong partnerships with businesses and community organizations are crucial for the sustainability and growth of Steampreneurship programs. These partnerships can provide real-world projects for students, internship opportunities, and funding or resources to support the programs. Engaging industry partners also ensures that the curriculum remains relevant to current market needs and technological advancements.

Securing Sustainable Funding: Sustainability is a significant challenge for any educational program that requires resources beyond the traditional classroom setup. Securing funding through grants, educational endowments, or partnerships is essential. Additionally, developing a clear value proposition for Steampreneurship programs will help attract investment from stakeholders who are interested in the long-term benefits of fostering a skilled and adaptable workforce.

Ongoing Research and Adaptation: As Steampreneurship programs expand, continuous research is necessary to assess their effectiveness and adapt the approach based on feedback and changing educational needs. This research should focus not only on academic outcomes but also on long-term career success and satisfaction among Steampreneurship graduates.

Steampreneurship represents a forward-thinking approach to education that aligns closely with the needs of today's students and tomorrow's workforce. By advocating for its expansion and strategically planning for its sustainability and scalability, stakeholders can ensure that the benefits of Steampreneurship reach a wide array of students, equipping them with the skills necessary to navigate and thrive in an increasingly complex and dynamic world.

~ 7 ~

MEASURING SUCCESS AND SCALABILTY

Evaluation Techniques

Defining Metrics for Success

Learning Outcomes

To measure the success of Steampreneurship through Inter-disciplinary Experiential Entrepreneurship programs effectively, it is essential to establish clear and comprehensive metrics that reflect the cognitive, emotional, and practical skills students acquire. These metrics serve as benchmarks for evaluating the impact of Steampreneurship and guiding future improvements.

Cognitive Skills:

Critical Thinking and Problem-Solving Capabilities: Assess students' ability to analyze complex problems, evaluate solutions, and make decisions using structured tools like rubrics that rate analytical thinking and problem-solving steps.

Entrepreneurial Mindset: Measure the development of an entrepreneurial mindset through pre- and post-program surveys that assess traits such as initiative, risk-taking, and adaptability.

Emotional Skills:

Resilience and Perseverance: Track changes in students' resilience and their ability to persevere through challenges. This can be measured through self-reporting tools and observational assessments by educators.

Empathy and Social Awareness: Evaluate students' growth in empathy and social awareness, crucial for social entrepreneurship, using reflective essays and peer feedback.

Practical Skills:

Project Execution and Management: Assess students' competence in managing and executing projects from conception to completion. This includes their ability to plan, organize resources, collaborate with peers, and achieve project goals.

Real-World Application: Monitor the application of theoretical knowledge in real-world scenarios through performance-based assessments and feedback from external partners involved in student projects.

Research Support

Evidence-Based Evaluation:

Established Educational Frameworks: Utilize established educational evaluation frameworks such as Bloom's Taxonomy for cognitive skills and SEL (Social and Emotional Learning) frameworks for emotional skills to ensure that assessments are robust and comprehensive.

Alignment with Educational Standards: Align metrics with national and international educational standards to ensure that they are rigorous, relevant, and recognized across educational settings.

Empirical Studies:

Research by Prince (2004) highlights the effectiveness of active learning techniques, including experiential learning, in enhancing problem-solving skills and technical abilities in students. Prince's study can guide the development of problem-solving metrics in Steampreneurship programs.

According to Dweck (2007), fostering a growth mindset is crucial for developing resilience and adaptability, important aspects of the entrepreneurial mindset. Dweck's findings support the inclusion of mindset-oriented assessments in evaluating emotional outcomes of Steampreneurship.

Quantitative and Qualitative Measures

To comprehensively assess the impact of Steampreneurship through Interdisciplinary Experiential Entrepreneurship programs, it is essential to employ a dual approach that incorporates both quantitative and qualitative measures. This balanced methodology ensures a robust evaluation of program effectiveness, capturing both the measurable outcomes and the nuanced experiences of participants.

Quantitative Data

Test Scores:

Measure improvements in students' knowledge and skills before and after participation in Steampreneurship programs using standardized tests or custom assessments designed specifically for the program.

Project Completion Rates:

Track the number of projects successfully completed by students, which reflects their ability to apply what they have learned in a practical setting and manage projects effectively.

Startup Success Rates:

For programs that encourage students to launch their own ventures, measure the success rates of these startups, which could include metrics like profitability, sustainability, or market penetration.

Qualitative Feedback

Student Reflections:

Collect and analyze student reflections on their learning experiences, challenges faced, and skills developed through the program. These reflections provide insights into the personal growth and engagement of students with the Steampreneurship curriculum.

Teacher Observations:

Gather feedback from teachers regarding student progress, the applicability of Steampreneurship methods, and the overall impact on students' learning and development. Teachers' perspectives are invaluable as they observe students' journeys throughout the program.

Stakeholder Reviews:

Include feedback from all stakeholders involved in the Steampreneurship program, such as industry partners, community leaders, and parents. Their reviews can offer external perspectives on the program's effectiveness and its impact on the community.

Research Support

Effectiveness of Mixed Methods:

According to Greene et al. (1989), combining quantitative and qualitative research methods provides a more comprehensive understanding of educational impacts by addressing both the extent of change and the nature of the change experienced by participants.

A study by Creswell and Plano Clark (2007) supports the use of mixed methods in educational research as it helps in validating and corroborating findings across different types of data, offering a more nuanced evaluation of program effectiveness.

Assessment Tools and Methods

To effectively measure the impact of Steampreneurship through Interdisciplinary Experiential Entrepreneurship programs, it is crucial to employ strategic assessment tools and methods that capture both the immediate and long-term effects of the educational interventions. These assessments help to quantify the benefits, guide continuous improvement, and substantiate the value of Steampreneurship programs to stakeholders.

Pre and Post Evaluations

Implementation Strategy:

Pre-Evaluation: Before initiating Steampreneurship interventions, administer baseline assessments to students to gauge their initial knowledge and skill levels. This could involve standardized tests, skill assessments, and surveys that measure various competencies and mindsets relevant to entrepreneurship and interdisciplinary learning.

Post-Evaluation: After the completion of the Steampreneurship program, conduct the same assessments to measure any changes in students' knowledge, skills, and attitudes. The comparison between pre- and post-intervention data provides a clear measure of the learning gains attributed to the program.

Benefits of Pre and Post Evaluations:

Direct Impact Analysis: This method allows educators to directly measure the educational impact of Steampreneurship interventions on students by providing concrete data on how much students have learned and grown during the program.

Customizable Assessment Tools: Schools can tailor these evaluations to reflect the specific objectives of their Steampreneurship programs, ensuring that they are measuring what is most relevant to their educational goals.

Longitudinal Studies

Study Design:
Tracking Over Time: Longitudinal studies involve following the same group of students over an extended period, from their participation in the Steampreneurship program through various stages of their educational and professional careers.

Data Collection Points: Collect data at multiple intervals post-intervention, such as immediately after the program, one year later, and five years later, to assess the sustained impacts of the education received.

Key Metrics:
Career Success: Measure indicators of career success, such as employment rates, entrepreneurship rates, career advancement, and professional achievements, among alumni of the Steampreneurship programs.

Real-World Impact: Evaluate the real-world impacts of the skills and knowledge acquired through Steampreneurship, such as the success of businesses started by alumni, their contributions to innovation, and their roles in community and economic development.

Benefits of Longitudinal Studies:

Depth of Insight: These studies provide a deeper understanding of the long-term effectiveness of Steampreneurship by showing how it influences career trajectories and long-term success.

Evidence of Sustainability: Longitudinal data helps educators and policymakers understand whether the skills imparted through Steampreneurship are enduring and continually beneficial in the rapidly changing global economy.

Research Support

Validation of Assessment Methods:

Immediate Learning Outcomes: Research by Kirkpatrick and Kirkpatrick (2006) supports the use of pre and post evaluations as effective tools for measuring learning outcomes in educational programs. They provide a straightforward method to assess immediate training effectiveness.

Long-Term Impact: According to studies by Baxter and Jack (2008), longitudinal qualitative research is crucial for understanding the lasting impact of educational interventions and providing a comprehensive view of their outcomes.

Stakeholder Feedback: Fostering Continuous Improvement

In the realm of education, stakeholder feedback serves as a compass, guiding the trajectory of programs and initiatives towards greater efficacy and relevance. When implementing Steampreneurship through Interdisciplinary Experiential Entrepreneurship in schools, soliciting feedback from all stakeholders is paramount to ensure that the program meets the needs and expectations of those it serves. This section explores the various methods of gathering stakeholder feedback, ranging from regular surveys to in-depth case studies, and highlights their significance in driving continuous improvement within the Steampreneurship framework.

Regular Surveys: A Pulse on Perceptions

Frequency and Scope: Regular surveys conducted throughout the academic year provide a pulse on stakeholders' perceptions of the Steampreneurship program. These surveys should encompass all stakeholders, including students, teachers, industry partners, and parents, to capture a comprehensive range of perspectives.

Assessing Effectiveness:

Student Engagement: Surveys aimed at students can gauge their level of engagement with Steampreneurship activities, their perceptions of the relevance of the content, and their overall satisfaction with the program.

Educator Perspectives: Teachers' feedback is invaluable in assessing the effectiveness of instructional strategies, the adequacy of resources and support, and the integration of Steampreneurship principles into the curriculum.

Industry Partnerships: Feedback from industry partners helps evaluate the alignment between the skills students acquire through Steampreneurship and the demands of the workforce, ensuring that the program remains relevant and responsive to industry needs.

Parental Involvement: Parents' perceptions of Steampreneurship can shed light on their understanding of the program's objectives, their satisfaction with their child's educational experience, and their support for continued participation.

Tailoring Surveys:

Customization: Surveys should be tailored to the specific roles and expectations of each stakeholder group, ensuring that the questions resonate with their experiences and priorities.

Anonymous Responses: To encourage candid feedback, surveys can be anonymized to allow stakeholders to express their opinions freely without fear of repercussion.

Research Support:

Research by Marsh et al. (2009) highlights the effectiveness of regular stakeholder surveys in providing actionable insights for improving educational programs. Their study emphasizes the importance of incorporating diverse stakeholder perspectives to gain a comprehensive understanding of program impact.

Case Studies: Learning from Successes and Challenges

Detailed Documentation: Case studies offer a qualitative lens through which to examine the intricacies of Steampreneurship projects, documenting successes, challenges, and lessons learned along the way. These narratives provide rich insights into the application of entrepreneurial principles in real-world contexts.

Key Components of Case Studies:

Project Objectives: Each case study should begin by outlining the objectives of the project, including the problem statement, goals, and desired outcomes.

Implementation Details: Detailed descriptions of how the project was executed, including the methodologies employed, the roles of various stakeholders, and any unforeseen obstacles encountered.

Outcomes and Impact: Case studies should evaluate the outcomes of the project against the initial objectives, highlighting areas of success as well as areas for improvement.

Reflections and Recommendations: Finally, each case study should include reflections from participants and recommendations for future iterations of similar projects.

Benefits of Case Studies:

Learning Opportunities: By examining both successful and unsuccessful projects, students can glean valuable insights into effective problem-solving strategies, collaboration techniques, and entrepreneurial mindset.

Informing Program Design: Educators and program administrators can use the findings from case studies to refine curriculum design, adjust instructional approaches, and identify areas for additional support or resources.

Research Support:
Case studies have been widely employed in educational research as a method for documenting the implementation and outcomes of innovative educational programs. Studies by Yin (2017) and Stake (2005) underscore the value of case studies in providing context-rich insights into complex educational phenomena.

Regular surveys and case studies serve as indispensable tools for gathering stakeholder feedback and driving continuous improvement within the Steampreneurship framework. By actively soliciting and analyzing feedback from students, teachers, industry partners, and parents, educators can ensure that the program remains responsive to evolving needs and aspirations. Moreover, detailed case studies offer illuminating snapshots of the real-world application of Steampreneurship principles, fostering a culture of reflective practice and innovation within educational settings.

Scaling Globally

Adapting Steampreneurship for Diverse Educational Settings

As Steampreneurship through Interdisciplinary Experiential Entrepreneurship gains traction, the challenge of scaling it globally requires a thoughtful approach to adaptation, particularly with respect to cultural diversity. Integrating Steampreneurship into various educational systems around the world demands not only a transfer of knowledge and methodologies but also a deep respect and understanding of local cultural norms and values. This section explores strategies for culturally adapting Steampreneurship to enhance its global acceptance and effectiveness.

Cultural Adaptation

Understanding Local Contexts:
Cultural Sensitivity: Before introducing Steampreneurship into a new cultural setting, it is essential to conduct thorough

research to understand the local educational norms, values, and practices. This understanding helps in modifying the Steampreneurship curriculum to align with local expectations and ways of learning.

Community Engagement: Engaging with local educators, community leaders, and other stakeholders is crucial for gaining insights into the cultural nuances that might affect the implementation of Steampreneurship. This engagement also helps in building trust and collaboration, which are fundamental for the successful adoption of any educational innovation.

Curriculum Modifications:

Content Localization: Adapt the content of Steampreneurship programs to include local case studies, examples, and references that resonate with the students' everyday experiences and cultural backgrounds. For instance, entrepreneurial projects could be tailored to address local community needs or opportunities.

Language Adaptation: Where necessary, translate materials and deliver instruction in the local language to ensure accessibility and comprehension. Additionally, consider the cultural connotations of translations to avoid misinterpretations that could alter the content's intended meaning.

Pedagogical Adjustments:

Teaching Methods: Different cultures have different learning styles and classroom dynamics. For example, some cultures emphasize group harmony and collective learning, while others value individualism and competitive achievements. Understanding these differences is key to adapting teaching methods and classroom management techniques.

Instructor Training: Equip local educators with the necessary training to deliver Steampreneurship effectively within their cultural context. This includes not only the pedagogical skills but also an understanding of how to integrate Steampreneurship principles with sensitivity to cultural nuances.

Research Support

Empirical Evidence:

Cultural Compatibility in Education: Research by Hofstede (1986) on cultural dimensions demonstrates that educational strategies that align with local cultural dimensions are more likely to be successful. This finding supports the need for cultural adaptation in the global scaling of Steampreneurship.

Effectiveness of Localized Learning: Studies by Gay (2000) on culturally responsive teaching highlight the positive impacts of adapting teaching practices to the cultural contexts of students, including increased student engagement and better learning outcomes.

Scaling Globally

Infrastructure Variability

When scaling Steampreneurship through Interdisciplinary Experiential Entrepreneurship globally, it is imperative to acknowledge and adapt to the varying infrastructural realities of different regions. Infrastructure, in terms of educational facilities, technological availability, and access to resources, significantly influences the implementation and success of educational programs. Understanding and addressing these variations is crucial for the effective global deployment of Steampreneurship.

Understanding Infrastructure Variability

Assessment of Local Infrastructure:

Technology Access: Assess the availability and reliability of technological infrastructure, including internet connectivity, computer labs, and digital learning tools, which are essential for many Steampreneurship activities.

Educational Facilities: Evaluate the physical educational facilities to determine how well they can support Steampreneurship initiatives, such as space for team projects or resources for building prototypes.

Resource Availability: Identify the availability of both human and material resources necessary for Steampreneurship, such as qualified instructors, industry experts, and materials for experiential learning activities.

Strategic Adaptations:

Customizing Technology Use: In regions with limited technological infrastructure, adapt Steampreneurship programs to rely less on digital tools and more on physical and interactive learning experiences that can be facilitated without high-tech equipment.

Resource-Based Adjustments: In areas with resource constraints, modify Steampreneurship projects and activities to utilize locally available materials and human resources, ensuring that the programs are sustainable and not dependent on external supplies.

Infrastructure-Specific Implementation Strategies

Low-Technology Solutions:

Paper-Based and Community-Driven Approaches: In areas with minimal access to technology, use paper-based resources or leverage community resources for learning. For instance, local businesses and markets can be used as real-world learning environments for entrepreneurship projects.

Utilizing Local Expertise: Where access to formal educational resources is limited, incorporate local business leaders and entrepreneurs as guest instructors or mentors, enriching the program with practical insights and real-world relevance.

High-Technology Environments:

Integrating Advanced Technologies: In regions with advanced technological infrastructure, fully integrate tools like virtual reality, online collaboration platforms, and advanced simulation software to enhance the experiential learning aspect of Steampreneurship.

Continuous Online Learning Opportunities: Leverage high-speed internet and digital platforms to offer continuous learning and development opportunities outside the classroom, such as webinars, online courses, and virtual mentoring.

Research Support

Effective Adaptation to Infrastructure:

A study by Unwin et al. (2010) emphasizes the importance of adapting educational interventions to local infrastructural conditions to enhance the effectiveness and sustainability of educational programs.

Further research by Warschauer (2003) discusses how technology implementation in education should be contextually appropriate, suggesting that the mere presence of technology does not guarantee educational improvement but must be adapted to local educational and infrastructural contexts.

Strategies for Global Implementation: Partnership Development

As Steampreneurship through Interdisciplinary Experiential Entrepreneurship programs seek global expansion, the development of strategic partnerships becomes a cornerstone for their successful implementation. Collaborations with educational institutions, businesses, and non-governmental organizations (NGOs) across various regions can provide the necessary support, resources, and local insights critical for adapting and thriving in diverse educational landscapes.

Building Effective Partnerships

Educational Institutions:
Collaboration with Schools and Universities: Partnering with local schools, colleges, and universities can help integrate Steampreneurship into existing curricula and leverage the infrastructure and educational expertise of these institutions. Such partnerships can also facilitate teacher exchanges or joint research projects to foster innovation in educational methods.

Accreditation and Certification Programs: Develop partnerships that allow for the accreditation of Steampreneurship courses, enhancing their credibility and appeal. This could involve collaborating with educational accreditation bodies to ensure that Steampreneurship programs meet local and international educational standards.

Businesses:
Industry Engagement: Form alliances with local and international businesses to provide students with real-world exposure and internship opportunities. These partnerships can also

involve businesses as sponsors, providing financial support or resources for Steampreneurship initiatives.

Mentorship Programs: Collaborate with business leaders to establish mentorship programs where students can receive guidance, business insights, and career advice, enriching the experiential learning process.

Non-Governmental Organizations (NGOs):

Community Projects: Partner with NGOs to design and implement community-oriented projects that allow students to apply entrepreneurial solutions to real-world social, environmental, or economic challenges. These projects not only enhance learning but also contribute to societal improvement.

Global Outreach: NGOs with a global presence can help facilitate the introduction of Steampreneurship programs in underprivileged areas, expanding educational opportunities and fostering global citizenship among students.

Research Support

Benefits of Educational Partnerships:

According to Bjorklund and Krämer (2019), partnerships between educational institutions and industry can significantly enhance educational outcomes by providing students with practical experiences and access to professional networks, thereby improving job readiness.

A study by Saxena (2014) emphasizes the role of NGOs in education, highlighting how their involvement can extend educational resources to marginalized communities, promoting inclusivity and diversity in learning.

Training and Support Systems

For the global expansion of Steampreneurship through Interdisciplinary Experiential Entrepreneurship programs to succeed, it is essential to establish comprehensive training systems for local educators and provide ongoing support. These initiatives ensure that the program's integrity and effectiveness are maintained across different cultural and educational contexts.

Establishing Comprehensive Training Systems

Development of Training Modules:

Curriculum-Specific Training: Develop training modules that are specifically tailored to the Steampreneurship curriculum, ensuring that educators are well-versed in both the theoretical and practical aspects of the program. These modules should cover the pedagogical approaches unique to experiential and entrepreneurial education.

Cultural Sensitivity Training: Include training components that focus on cultural sensitivity and adaptation, helping educators to effectively engage with students from diverse backgrounds and tailor the curriculum to local cultural norms.

Delivery Mechanisms:

Online Platforms: Utilize online learning platforms to deliver training modules, making it accessible to educators in different regions. This approach also allows for the integration of interactive elements such as webinars, virtual classrooms, and discussion forums.

In-Person Workshops: Conduct in-person training sessions, especially in regions where face-to-face interaction is more effective or preferred. These workshops can also serve as networking opportunities for educators to share insights and best practices.

Providing Ongoing Support

Mentorship Programs:

Experienced Educators as Mentors: Establish a mentorship program where experienced Steampreneurship educators mentor new instructors. This one-on-one guidance helps new teachers navigate the initial challenges of implementing Steampreneurship and enhances their teaching efficacy.

Peer Support Networks: Create networks of Steampreneurship educators across different regions to foster a community of practice. These networks can facilitate the exchange of ideas, resources, and support, reinforcing the program's global community.

Continuous Professional Development:

Update Training: Regularly update training content to reflect the latest research, technological advancements, and pedagogical strategies. This ensures that educators remain at the forefront of experiential and entrepreneurial education.

Feedback-Driven Improvements: Implement a system for collecting and analyzing feedback from educators about the training and support they receive. Use this feedback to continuously improve the training and support services offered.

Research Support

Effectiveness of Educator Training:

According to Desimone (2009), effective professional development for teachers significantly improves their teaching skills and students' educational outcomes. Desimone's work emphasizes the importance of content-focused, active learning in professional development.

A study by Darling-Hammond et al. (2017) supports the need for ongoing professional development and mentorship in maintaining high educational standards and teacher satisfaction.

$\sim 8 \sim$

CONTINUOUS IMPROVEMENT

Feedback Mechanisms

The dynamism of Steampreneurship through Interdisciplinary Experiential Entrepreneurship necessitates an environment of continuous improvement, supported by robust feedback mechanisms. Iterative feedback loops are essential for refining and enhancing the Steampreneurship curriculum, teaching methods, and student outcomes, adapting in real-time to the evolving educational landscape and the specific needs of students and educators.

Iterative Feedback Loops

Designing Effective Feedback Systems:
Real-Time Data Collection: Implement tools and processes that allow for the continuous collection of feedback throughout the duration of Steampreneurship projects. This could include

digital surveys, mobile apps for instant feedback, and interactive online platforms where students and teachers can comment on their experiences and outcomes.

Stakeholder Engagement: Regularly engage all stakeholders —including students, educators, industry partners, and parents —in the feedback process. This broad inclusion ensures diverse perspectives are considered in evaluating the program's effectiveness and areas for improvement.

Feedback Integration into Curriculum Development:

Rapid Response Systems: Develop systems that allow curriculum developers and educators to quickly integrate feedback into the educational process. This could involve having dedicated teams to analyze feedback and propose adjustments to the curriculum or teaching strategies in near real-time.

Scheduled Review Sessions: In addition to real-time adjustments, establish regular review sessions (e.g., quarterly or bi-annually) where more substantial curriculum revisions can be discussed and implemented based on accumulated feedback.

Utilizing Technology for Feedback Collection

Digital Feedback Tools:

Learning Management Systems (LMS): Use the capabilities of LMS platforms to gather ongoing feedback on course content, teaching methods, and student engagement. Features such as forums, polls, and analytics provide a wealth of data that can be used to assess and enhance the learning experience.

Analytics and Reporting Tools: Leverage advanced analytics tools to interpret large datasets of feedback, identifying trends, patterns, and outliers that can inform more targeted improvements.

Research Support

The Impact of Feedback on Educational Programs:

Research by Hattie and Timperley (2007) emphasizes the significant role of effective feedback in enhancing student achievement. Their framework outlines how feedback should be timely, relevant, and action-oriented to positively influence student learning.

A study by Boud and Molloy (2013) highlights the importance of using feedback not just for assessment of learning but as a tool for continuous improvement and active learning engagement.

Annual Reviews

Annual review sessions are a pivotal component of the continuous improvement process for Steampreneurship through Interdisciplinary Experiential Entrepreneurship programs. These sessions provide an opportunity to collectively reflect on the year's achievements and challenges, allowing educators, students, and other stakeholders to discuss and strategize on the future direction of the program.

Conducting Annual Reviews

Structured Review Sessions:

Inclusive Participation: Ensure that all stakeholders, including educators, students, industry partners, and parents, are invited to participate in the review sessions. This inclusive approach ensures that the program receives diverse perspectives, enriching the feedback and making the improvements more comprehensive and impactful.

Data-Driven Discussions: Prepare for the sessions by collecting data throughout the year on various aspects of the program, such as student performance, project outcomes, and stakeholder satisfaction. This data should be presented in an accessible format to facilitate informed discussions during the review sessions.

Focus Areas for Review:

Curriculum Effectiveness: Assess the relevance and impact of the curriculum on students' learning and development. Identify subjects or modules that were particularly successful and those that require revision.

Teaching Methods: Evaluate the effectiveness of teaching methods and educational tools used throughout the year. Consider feedback on what methods engaged students most effectively and which areas need new strategies or resources.

Stakeholder Engagement: Discuss the level and quality of engagement from all stakeholders, identifying successful collaborations and areas where greater involvement or support is needed.

Resource Allocation: Review the allocation of resources, including funding, materials, and human resources, to determine if they have been optimally utilized and plan for future resource needs.

Leveraging Feedback for Improvement

Actionable Insights:
Development of Action Plans: Based on the discussions and feedback received during the review sessions, develop concrete action plans to address identified issues. These plans should outline specific steps, responsible parties, and timelines for implementation.

Monitoring Progress: Establish mechanisms to monitor the implementation of action plans throughout the coming year, ensuring that the changes are effective and adjusting the plans as necessary based on ongoing feedback and results.

Research Support

Importance of Reflective Practices in Education:

A study by Boud, Keogh, and Walker (1985) emphasizes the significance of reflection in learning processes, suggesting that structured reflection enhances learning outcomes by helping learners internalize and apply feedback.

Schön (1983) also highlights the role of reflective practice in improving professional activities by continuously questioning and refining practices in light of new experiences and information.

Incorporating Technological Advances

In the rapidly evolving landscape of education technology, staying current is crucial for maintaining the effectiveness and relevance of Steampreneurship through Interdisciplinary Experiential Entrepreneurship programs. By regularly updating technological tools and employing advanced data analytics, Steampreneurshipcan enhance its educational offerings and adapt to the changing needs of students and the marketplace.

Technology Integration

Updating Technological Tools:

Assessment of Current Technologies: Conduct annual reviews of the existing technological tools used in Steampreneurship programs to assess their effectiveness and relevance. This includes evaluating software, hardware, and online resources.

Incorporating New Technologies: Stay informed about the latest advancements in educational technology and assess their potential integration into the Steampreneurship curriculum. This could involve adopting new learning management systems, virtual reality (VR) environments, or artificial intelligence (AI) tools that enhance interactive learning.

Training and Support: Provide ongoing training for educators and technical support to ensure that the integration of new technologies is smooth and that all users are competent in utilizing these tools effectively.

Enhancing Learning Experiences:

Interactive Platforms: Utilize platforms that facilitate interactive learning and collaboration among students, such as augmented reality (AR) apps or collaborative project management tools that simulate real-world business scenarios.

Customized Learning Paths: Implement adaptive learning technologies that tailor educational content to the needs of individual students based on their learning pace and style, thereby optimizing the learning experience for each student.

Data Analytics

Advanced Data Collection and Analysis:

Collection of Comprehensive Data: Utilize tools and methodologies that allow for the collection of detailed data on student performance, engagement, and outcomes. This includes the use of sensors, log data from digital platforms, and feedback mechanisms integrated into educational apps and platforms.

Analysis of Trends and Patterns: Employ sophisticated data analytics tools to analyze the collected data, identify trends and patterns, and gain insights into the effectiveness of teaching methods and curriculum design.

Predictive Analytics and Decision Making:

Predictive Modeling: Use predictive analytics to forecast student outcomes based on current or historical data. This can help in identifying at-risk students early and adjusting teaching strategies or support mechanisms to better cater to their needs.

Informing Program Adjustments: Leverage the insights gained from data analytics to make informed decisions about curriculum adjustments, teaching methods, and resource allocation. This data-driven approach ensures that changes are based on solid evidence and likely to improve program effectiveness.

Research Support

The Role of Technology in Enhancing Education:
According to a study by Picciano (2017), the integration of technology in educational settings has shown significant improvements in student engagement and learning outcomes, particularly when technologies are used strategically to enhance interactive learning and personalized education.

Research by Siemens and Baker (2012) on the use of data analytics in education highlights the potential of this technology to transform educational practices by enabling more informed decisions and personalized learning experiences.

Research and Development

To ensure that Steampreneurship through Interdisciplinary Experiential Entrepreneurship remains effective and cutting-edge, ongoing research and development must be integral components of the program. These activities not only keep the curriculum and teaching methods current but also validate the efficacy of Steampreneurship through empirical evidence, ensuring that it continues to meet the needs of students in diverse educational contexts.

Ongoing Research

Purpose and Focus:

Innovation in Education: Continuously explore new educational theories, methods, and technologies that could enhance the Steampreneurshipcurriculum. This involves staying abreast of the latest research findings and trends in education, particularly in experiential learning and entrepreneurship education.

Efficacy and Adaptation: Regularly assess and refine the Steampreneurship program based on rigorous academic research. This includes studying the impact of Steampreneurship on student outcomes, such as academic performance, career readiness, and personal development.

Research Methods:

Empirical Studies: Conduct empirical studies to test the effectiveness of different components of the Steampreneurshipcurriculum. This could involve experimental designs, longitudinal studies, and case studies.

Collaborative Research: Engage in collaborative research efforts with universities, think tanks, and other educational institutions. These partnerships can enhance the depth and breadth of research capabilities and provide a wider range of insights and data.

Utilization of Research Findings:

Curriculum Development: Integrate findings from ongoing research directly into curriculum design and teaching practices, ensuring that the Steampreneurshipprogram is grounded in proven educational principles and practices.

Policy and Practice: Use research outcomes to influence educational policy and practice, both within the institution and in the broader educational community. This helps in advocating for the wider adoption of experiential and entrepreneurship education.

Pilot Testing

Implementation of Pilot Programs:

Testing New Methods: Before rolling out new methods or tools on a wider scale, implement pilot programs to test these innovations in controlled, real-world educational settings. This allows for the assessment of their practicality and effectiveness.

Feedback and Iteration: Gather detailed feedback from participants and observers involved in the pilot programs. Use this feedback to make iterative improvements to the methods or tools being tested.

Benefits of Pilot Testing:

Risk Mitigation: Pilot testing helps mitigate the risks associated with implementing untested educational innovations. By identifying potential issues and challenges in a smaller, controlled environment, necessary adjustments can be made before full-scale implementation.

Stakeholder Confidence: Successfully conducted pilot tests can build confidence among stakeholders, including educators, students, and funders, about the viability and potential success of new initiatives.

Research Support

Educational Research Foundations:

A study by Freeman et al. (2014) underscores the value of active learning in improving student performance in science, technology, engineering, and math (STEM) fields. This research supports the emphasis on active, experiential learning methods in Steampreneurship.

Research by Kuh (2008) on high-impact educational practices provides evidence that experiential learning practices, such as those used in Steampreneurship, significantly enhance student engagement and learning outcomes.

~ 9 ~

STEAMPRENEURSHIP THE FUTURE OF EDUCATION

Trends and Predictions: Steampreneurship's Role in the Future Educational Landscape

In the rapidly evolving world of education, the paradigm is shifting from traditional teaching methods towards more dynamic, student-centered learning. Steampreneurship is at the forefront of this transformation, aligning perfectly with the emerging trends of lifelong learning and the customization of educational experiences to individual needs. This section explores how Steampreneurship not only meets these evolving educational demands but also sets the stage for future developments in the educational landscape.

Lifelong Learning

The Necessity of Continuous Education:

Career Fluidity: In today's fast-paced global economy, career paths are no longer linear. Individuals are likely to change professions multiple times throughout their lives, necessitating continuous education and skill development. Steampreneurship's focus on developing core competencies like critical thinking, adaptability, and problem-solving prepares individuals to thrive in various fields and adapt to new careers as they emerge.

Self-Directed Learning: Steampreneurship promotes self-directed learning that empowers individuals to take control of their educational journeys. This approach fosters a lifelong learning habit that extends beyond formal education into personal and professional development.

Research Support:

According to a study by Jenkins and Mostafa (2015), lifelong learning and continuous professional development significantly contribute to career success and satisfaction. Steampreneurship's emphasis on entrepreneurial skills aligns with these findings, supporting the argument that such skills are crucial for navigating the modern job market.

Customization and Personalization

Meeting Individual Needs:

Tailored Learning Experiences: With the advent of big data and advanced analytics, educational programs can now be tailored to the specific learning styles and paces of individual students. Steampreneurship leverages these technologies to customize projects and learning modules, ensuring that each student can engage with the material in the most effective way possible.

Responsive Curriculum: Steampreneurship's project-based learning model is inherently flexible, allowing educators to adjust content and projects based on ongoing assessment and feedback. This responsiveness ensures that educational experiences are relevant to students' interests and career aspirations, enhancing engagement and efficacy.

Research Support:

A meta-analysis by Bernard et al. (2014) highlights the positive impacts of individualized learning approaches on student achievement across various educational settings. The research supports the implementation of personalized learning environments in Steampreneurship, underscoring their effectiveness in improving educational outcomes.

Furthermore, studies by the Institute for the Future (2017) predict that personalization in education will become increasingly important as technology allows for more individualized learning experiences.

The Future Landscape

Integrating Steampreneurship into Mainstream Education:

Policy Advocacy: To facilitate the widespread adoption of Steampreneurship, advocacy for educational policy changes that support personalized, lifelong learning is crucial. This includes funding for technologies that enable personalization, professional development for educators in experiential learning methods, and recognition of Steampreneurship credentials in both academic and professional settings.

Global Standardization: While customization is key, there is also a need for standardizing certain core elements of Steampreneurship to ensure consistency and transferability of skills across different regions and industries. Developing global standards for experiential and entrepreneurial education can help achieve this balance.

Steampreneurship is not just a teaching method but a necessary evolution in the educational sector that addresses the current and future needs of students worldwide. By fostering skills that are critical for lifelong success and adapting to the unique needs of each learner, Steampreneurship offers a robust model for education that prepares individuals not only for the jobs of today but for adapting to the careers of tomorrow.

Trends and Predictions: Technological Integration in Steampreneurship

As Steampreneurship aligns with future educational trends, the integration of advanced technologies such as Artificial Intelligence (AI), automation, Virtual Reality (VR), and Augmented Reality (AR) plays a pivotal role. These technologies not only enhance the learning experience but also streamline educational processes, allowing educators to focus more on pedagogy and less on administrative duties. This section explores the transformative potential of these technologies in revolutionizing Steampreneurship.

AI and Automation in Education

Enhancing Efficiency and Effectiveness:

Automation of Administrative Tasks: AI and automation are increasingly being employed to handle time-consuming administrative tasks such as attendance, grading, and scheduling. By automating these processes, educators can devote more time to interactive teaching and personalized student interactions, which are core to the Steampreneurship philosophy.

Personalized Learning Paths: AI algorithms can analyze individual student performance and learning styles to tailor educational content, thus enhancing the personalization aspect of Steampreneurship. This technology allows for the adjustment of curriculum pacing and complexity based on real-time student data, ensuring optimal learning outcomes for each student.

Predictive Analytics:

Identifying Learning Gaps: AI can be used to predict student performance and identify potential learning gaps before they become problematic. This capability enables preemptive educational interventions that can significantly improve learning efficacy and student achievement.

Enhancing Student Retention: Through predictive analytics, institutions can also monitor and boost student engagement and retention, crucial metrics in educational success, especially in more dynamic and demanding programs like Steampreneurship.

Research Support:
A study by Zhou et al. (2020) highlights the significant time savings and reduction in workload for teachers through the use of AI in administrative tasks, allowing more focus on teaching and student engagement.

Research by Baker and Smith (2019) demonstrated that AI-driven personalized learning significantly improved student performance, particularly in complex subjects integrated within Steampreneurship curricula.

Virtual and Augmented Reality: Transforming Experiential Learning

Virtual Reality (VR):
Immersive Learning Environments: VR can create highly immersive and interactive environments that simulate real-world scenarios, which is invaluable in experiential learning contexts. For example, VR can transport students to virtual labs, historical sites, or even simulated business environments, providing experiential learning without the logistical constraints of physical field trips.

Enhanced Engagement and Retention: The immersive nature of VR has been shown to increase student engagement and information retention, particularly in subjects where practical experience is crucial for understanding complex concepts.

Augmented Reality (AR):

Enhancing Real-World Interactions: Unlike VR, AR enhances the real world by overlaying digital information onto the physical environment. In an Steampreneurship setting, AR can be used to bring abstract business concepts to life during lectures or overlay data and analytics onto physical objects, making the learning process both engaging and informative.

Collaborative Projects: AR also supports collaborative projects by allowing multiple users to interact with digital elements in a real-world context, facilitating teamwork and communication among students working on entrepreneurial projects.

Research Support:

A meta-analysis by Fernandez and Jamet (2021) found that VR significantly enhances learning outcomes in STEM education by providing immersive experiences that traditional educational methods cannot offer.

According to Johnson et al. (2019), AR has been effective in increasing student motivation and understanding in subjects requiring spatial awareness and hands-on learning, aligning well with Steampreneurship's focus on experiential learning.

Innovation in Education: Technologies and Methodologies Influencing Steampreneurship

Emerging Technologies: Blockchain in Education

As Steampreneurship through Interdisciplinary Experiential Entrepreneurship embraces future educational trends, blockchain technology emerges as a significant innovation. With its inherent qualities of transparency, security, and decentralization, blockchain holds transformative potential for educational systems, particularly in credentialing and the creation of new, decentralized educational models. This section delves into how blockchain can fundamentally alter the educational landscape, enhancing the integrity and flexibility of educational processes crucial to the success of Steampreneurship programs.

Blockchain's Role in Education

Securing Educational Credentials:
Immutable Records: Blockchain technology offers a robust solution for creating tamper-proof records of student achievements and credentials. By storing educational records on a blockchain, such as degrees, certificates, and transcripts, students and graduates gain a permanent, verifiable record of their accomplishments that can be easily shared with employers or educational institutions without the risk of falsification.

Ease of Verification: Blockchain simplifies the verification process for credentials, reducing the administrative burden on educational institutions and enhancing the trustworthiness of documents. This streamlined approach is particularly beneficial in a globalized education environment where students often need to prove their educational background across international borders.

Facilitating Decentralized Education Models:

Micro-credentialing and Badges: Blockchain technology enables the issuance of digital badges and micro-credentials, which are becoming increasingly popular in Steampreneurship and other modern educational paradigms. These credentials allow students to acquire and demonstrate smaller units of learning at their own pace, which are stackable towards larger qualifications.

Customized Learning Pathways: Through blockchain, educational providers can offer more flexible and personalized learning experiences. Students can curate their educational paths by selecting from a wide range of courses provided by different institutions, facilitated by the decentralized nature of blockchain.

Integration with Steampreneurship

Enhancing Experiential Learning:
Project Authentication: Blockchain can be used to authenticate the originality and ownership of student projects and intellectual property. This is especially relevant in Steampreneurship, where projects often involve innovative solutions and business ideas that may have commercial potential.

Real-Time Feedback and Assessment: Utilizing blockchain to record and track student performance and feedback continuously can enhance the experiential learning process. This transparent tracking system can help educators tailor educational interventions more effectively to student needs.

Research Support

Empirical Evidence:
A study by Sharples and Domingue (2016) explored the use of blockchain for recording student achievements and transferring

credits between institutions. Their findings suggest that block-chain technology not only increases efficiency and security but also supports a more learner-centered approach by giving students control over their educational records.

Research by Chen, et al. (2018) highlights the potential of blockchain in supporting lifelong learning through micro-credentials. Their work emphasizes how blockchain can facilitate seamless transitions between different educational stages and institutions, fostering an environment conducive to lifelong learning and professional development.

Data-Driven Personalization in Steampreneurship through Interdisciplinary Experiential Entrepreneurship

In the age of digital transformation, big data and analytics are revolutionizing the educational landscape, offering unprecedented opportunities for personalizing learning experiences. Steampreneurship through Interdisciplinary Experiential Entrepreneurship stands to benefit significantly from these technological advances, as they enable more tailored educational pathways that enhance student engagement and optimize learning outcomes. This section explores how leveraging big data and analytics can transform Steampreneurship by creating more individualized and effective educational experiences.

The Role of Big Data in Education

Understanding Big Data:

Definition and Scope: Big data in education refers to the vast amounts of information collected through digital learning platforms, online interactions, student performance tracking systems, and other educational technologies. This data encompasses everything from basic demographic information to detailed logs of student interactions with learning materials.

Application in Educational Settings:
Learning Analytics: By analyzing this extensive data, educators can gain insights into student learning habits, preferences, and challenges. Learning analytics involve the measurement, collection, analysis, and reporting of data about learners and their contexts, for purposes of understanding and optimizing learning and the environments in which it occurs.

Enhancing Steampreneurship with Data-Driven Personalization

Customized Learning Pathways:
Adaptive Learning Environments: Big data facilitates the creation of adaptive learning environments that adjust the difficulty level and the type of content presented based on individual student performance and engagement patterns. This adaptability ensures that each student is challenged appropriately and supported where necessary, which is crucial in experiential and entrepreneurship education.

Predictive Modeling: Utilizing predictive analytics, educators can forecast potential learning outcomes based on current trends. This allows for proactive adjustments to curricula and teaching strategies, potentially preventing student dropouts and enhancing educational achievements.

Enhanced Student Engagement:

Feedback and Recommendations: Automated systems can provide real-time feedback to students based on data-driven insights, offering personalized recommendations for additional resources, tutorials, or peer collaborations. This immediate response not only keeps students engaged but also ensures that their learning trajectory is continuously optimized.

Individualized Assessment Strategies:

Dynamic Assessment Models: Traditional assessment methods can be transformed by integrating data analytics to provide more dynamic, continuous assessments that reflect student progress in real time. These assessments are less about grading and more about providing ongoing feedback to enhance the learning process.

Research Support

Empirical Evidence:
Improved Learning Outcomes: A study by Baker and Siemens (2014) emphasizes the impact of data analytics on creating

personalized learning experiences that adapt to individual student needs, significantly improving engagement and academic performance.

Engagement and Retention: Research by Romero and Ventura (2013) demonstrates how data mining techniques can help in identifying disengaged students early in the process, allowing for timely interventions that improve retention rates.

Innovative Methodologies in Steampreneurship through Interdisciplinary Experiential Entrepreneurship

As educational paradigms shift to meet the demands of the 21st century, innovative methodologies such as flipped classrooms, blended learning, and gamification are becoming integral to enhancing student engagement and learning outcomes. These approaches are particularly well-suited to the principles of Steampreneurship through Interdisciplinary Experiential Entrepreneurship, which emphasizes hands-on learning and real-world applications. This section explores how these methodologies can be integrated into Steampreneurship to create a more dynamic and effective educational experience.

Flipped Classrooms and Blended Learning

Flipped Classrooms:

Concept and Implementation: In a flipped classroom model, traditional learning paradigms are inverted. Students first engage with new content outside of class, typically through video lectures or reading assignments. Classroom time is then dedicated to applying this knowledge through discussions, problem-solving sessions, and practical exercises. This method allows for greater interaction and personalized attention from the instructor during class time.

Integration with Steampreneurship: Flipped classrooms are particularly effective for Steampreneurship as they allow students to absorb theoretical knowledge at their own pace through pre-class activities and then apply this knowledge through collaborative projects and entrepreneurial ventures during class. This methodology supports the experiential learning aspect of Steampreneurship by maximizing the efficiency of classroom interaction and focusing on higher-level cognitive skills during school hours.

Blended Learning:

Hybrid Approach: Blended learning combines online educational materials and opportunities for interaction online with traditional place-based classroom methods. It requires the physical presence of both teacher and student, with some element of student control over time, place, path, or pace.

Benefits for Steampreneurship: Blended learning offers flexibility and a range of resources that can be particularly beneficial for Steampreneurship programs. It allows students to explore entrepreneurship concepts online while also benefiting from hands-on, guided instruction in the classroom. This flexibility can be crucial in accommodating the diverse needs of students pursuing entrepreneurial projects, which often require balancing theoretical input with practical execution.

Gamification in Education

Enhancing Engagement Through Game Elements:
Application of Gamification: Gamification involves applying game-design elements in non-game contexts to make learning activities more engaging and motivating. Elements such as point scoring, competitions, leaderboards, and achievement badges can transform an educational program like Steampreneurship into a more interactive and enjoyable experience.

Role in Steampreneurship: By introducing gamification into Steampreneurship, educators can enhance student motivation and engagement. For example, students can earn points for successfully completing project milestones or for innovative problem-solving, which can be tracked on a leaderboard. This not only motivates students through competition but also through the satisfaction of achieving visible rewards.

Research Support

Empirical Evidence:

Flipped Classroom Efficiency: A study by Abeysekera and Dawson (2015) found that flipped classrooms enhance student learning and engagement by allowing more time for active learning during class sessions. This methodology supports deeper understanding and application of complex concepts, such as those encountered in Steampreneurship.

Impact of Gamification: Research by Hamari, Koivisto, and Sarsa (2014) indicates that gamification leads to increased motivation and engagement in educational settings, making it an effective tool for enhancing student learning and involvement, particularly in areas requiring high levels of creativity and problem-solving.

Advocacy for Steampreneurship Adoption

In the quest to shape the future of education, advocating for supportive policies that encourage the widespread adoption of Steampreneurship through Interdisciplinary Experiential Entrepreneurship is crucial. These policies should not only aim to integrate Steampreneurship into mainstream educational systems but also ensure it is accessible to all, particularly underserved populations. By securing adequate funding and resources, Steampreneurship can be implemented effectively across diverse educational landscapes. This section outlines the policy advocacy necessary to achieve these goals, highlighting the benefits of educational equity and the importance of dedicated funding.

Policy Advocacy for Educational Equity

Bridging Educational Disparities with Steampreneurship:

Promoting Inclusivity: Steampreneurship offers a unique approach that can be particularly beneficial in addressing educational disparities. By advocating for policies that integrate Steampreneurship into public education systems, we can provide underserved students with opportunities to engage in hands-on, practical learning experiences that are often only available in more affluent educational settings.

Tailoring Education to Community Needs: Steampreneurship encourages learning that is deeply connected to real-world applications, which can be particularly meaningful in underserved areas. Policies should support the customization of Steampreneurship programs to address local community issues, thereby making education more relevant and impactful for students from all backgrounds.

Strategic Policy Recommendations:

Inclusive Curriculum Development: Advocate for the development and adoption of curricula that are inclusive of diverse cultural and socio-economic backgrounds. This involves ensuring that educational materials and project assignments within Steampreneurship programs are accessible and relatable to students from all walks of life.

Accessibility Measures: Push for policies that reduce barriers to entry for disadvantaged students, such as providing scholarships, transportation subsidies, and technology access to participate fully in Steampreneurship activities.

Funding and Resource Allocation

Necessity of Targeted Investment:

Governmental Support: Effective implementation of Steampreneurship requires substantial initial and ongoing investment. Advocating for governmental funding to support Steampreneurship programs is crucial. This includes funding for training educators, acquiring necessary technology and materials, and maintaining the infrastructure needed for experiential learning environments.

Private Sector Partnerships: Encourage partnerships with businesses and private foundations that can provide both funding and real-world expertise to Steampreneurship programs. These partnerships not only enhance the financial sustainability of Steampreneurship initiatives but also enrich the program content with industry-specific insights and opportunities for students.

Leveraging Steampreneurship for Economic Development:

Skill Development for Economic Growth: Highlight the role of Steampreneurship in developing entrepreneurial skills that are crucial for economic innovation and growth. Policies that support Steampreneurship can lead to the cultivation of a more entrepreneurial and skilled workforce, which is attractive for local and international businesses.

Creating Entrepreneurial Ecosystems: Advocate for the establishment of regional hubs or incubators that can foster innovation and entrepreneurship within the community, supported by Steampreneurship programs. These hubs can serve as catalysts for economic development and job creation, providing ongoing benefits beyond the educational sphere.

Research Support

Empirical Evidence:

A study by Scott-Clayton (2018) emphasizes the impact of targeted financial support on educational outcomes, particularly for students from low-income backgrounds. The research suggests that well-funded educational programs that offer experiential learning opportunities can significantly narrow achievement gaps.

Research by Ziegler et al. (2019) on the efficacy of experiential learning in fostering critical thinking and problem-solving skills underlines the importance of adequately resourced programs for maximizing educational benefits.

International Collaboration in Steampreneurship

In an increasingly interconnected world, fostering international collaboration in education is paramount. Steampreneurship through Interdisciplinary Experiential Entrepreneurship

(Steampreneurship) stands as a prime candidate for global integration, given its adaptability and focus on real-world skills. This section discusses the development of global standards for experiential learning and the promotion of cross-border educational programs that utilize Steampreneurship principles, thereby enhancing global citizenship and cross-cultural understanding.

Global Standards for Experiential Learning

Development of Global Standards:

Creating a Unified Framework: Propose the establishment of a comprehensive framework for experiential learning that can be adopted internationally. This framework would outline core competencies, pedagogical approaches, assessment methods, and best practices for implementing Steampreneurship. The aim is to ensure consistency and high quality in experiential learning across different educational systems and cultural contexts.

Collaborative Efforts: Engage international educational bodies, such as UNESCO and the International Baccalaureate Organization, to collaborate on the development of these standards. Their global reach and educational expertise make them ideal partners for spearheading such initiatives.

Benefits of Standardization:

Facilitating Mobility: Standardized frameworks make it easier for students to move between different educational systems without losing the value of their experiential learning achievements. This mobility is crucial in a globalized world where individuals increasingly work and study in multiple countries.

Enhancing Employability: By adhering to globally recognized standards, Steampreneurship programs help ensure that students acquire skills that are relevant and valued worldwide, thereby enhancing their employability and career prospects.

Research Support:

A study by Wagner (2015) highlights the importance of standardizing experiential learning practices to enhance their effectiveness and transferability across different learning environments. This research supports the notion that well-defined standards contribute to the broader acceptance and success of experiential learning methodologies.

Cross-border Educational Programs

Promoting International Educational Programs:

Steampreneurship Exchange Programs: Develop international exchange programs that allow students to engage in Steampreneurship projects in different countries. These programs would not only expose students to international business practices and challenges but also foster a deeper understanding of global markets and cultures.

Collaborative Projects: Encourage collaborative projects between students from different countries, facilitated through virtual platforms and occasional physical meet-ups. Such projects would tackle global issues, promoting a sense of global citizenship and responsibility.

Enhancing Cross-cultural Understanding:

Cultural Competence Training: Incorporate specific training sessions on cultural competence and communication within the Steampreneurship curriculum to prepare students for effective interaction in diverse international groups.

Global Problem Solving: Utilize Steampreneurship principles to address worldwide challenges, such as sustainability, healthcare, and education disparities. Engaging students from various backgrounds in these projects enhances their understanding of global issues and their ability to work across cultural divides.

Research Support:
According to research by Olson and Kroeger (2001), international collaborations in education significantly improve students' cultural sensitivities and adaptabilities. This study underlines the value of cross-border programs in fostering comprehensive educational experiences that are culturally aware and globally oriented.

Knight (2004) discusses the benefits of international learning networks and their role in promoting global citizenship and intercultural skills among students, further supporting the initiative for Steampreneurship-based international programs.

~ 10 ~

IMPLEMENTING STEAMPRENEURSHIP AT AA STEAM & ENTREPRENEURSHIP ACADEMY

Introduction: Vision for the Future

In an era marked by rapid technological advancements and global interconnectedness, the need for an educational model that not only keeps pace but leads the way in innovation and real-world applicability is more urgent than ever. AA Steam & Entrepreneurship Academy is my proposed vision to become a beacon of this new educational paradigm through its implementation of the Steampreneurship through Interdisciplinary Experiential Entrepreneurship curriculum. This final chapter outlines how the academy will bring this vision to life, offering a transformative educational experience designed to prepare students for the complexities of tomorrow's global economy.

Overview of AA Steam & Entrepreneurship Academy's Mission

AA Steam & Entrepreneurship Academy is founded on the principle that education should be a lever for empowerment, not just a preparatory stage for traditional career pathways. The academy's mission is to equip students from grades 4 through 12 with the skills and mindset necessary to navigate and shape the future. By integrating key academic subjects with the principles of entrepreneurship, the academy commits to fostering a generation of leaders who are innovative, economically savvy, and globally minded.

Rationale for Choosing Steampreneurship

The choice of Steampreneurship as the foundational curriculum framework for AA Steam & Entrepreneurship Academy stems from a critical evaluation of the current educational landscape, which often fails to connect theoretical learning with real-world applications. Traditional educational models have not kept pace with the dynamic economic and technological changes sweeping the globe. I have witnessed these gaps firsthand and was driven not only to critique but to create—leading to the charter proposal for an institution that addresses these shortcomings head-on.

Steampreneurship's relevance is particularly pronounced in today's economy where understanding global markets, sustainability, and technological integration is crucial. The curriculum is designed to make students not just participants in their education but active creators and thinkers, capable of launching viable businesses by applying what they learn in real-time, within a global context.

Implementing the Steampreneurship Curriculum

From Consumption to Creation:
At AA Steam & Entrepreneurship Academy, students will start their journey with an understanding of consumption—what they buy, use, and wear—and gradually learn to view these everyday items through the lens of global business and production. This foundational knowledge sets the stage for deeper explorations into business dynamics and market economies.

Business Creation and Entrepreneurial Days:

Each academic year, students will undertake the creation of two businesses, applying interdisciplinary skills from their courses in real-world contexts. These ventures will culminate in an Entrepreneur Day, where students will present their business projects to the community, showcasing their ability to innovate, market, and sell products or services. This not only reinforces their learning but also builds essential skills in leadership, financial literacy, and strategic thinking.

Grade-Level Progression:

As students advance from 4th to 12th grade, the complexity of their projects and the depth of their market analysis will increase. This progression is designed to continuously challenge students and expand their capabilities, ensuring that by the time they graduate, they have a solid understanding of business operations, market fluctuations, and the importance of sustainable practices.

Integration with Global Markets:

Understanding global supply chains and the economic impact of various industries will be a core element of the curriculum. Students will engage in projects that require them to trace products from conception to consumption, exploring international trade agreements, labor economics, and the environmental impacts of production and consumption.

Curriculum Design and Implementation

At AA Steam & Entrepreneurship Academy, the curriculum is designed to not only educate but to mold future leaders capable of understanding and influencing global markets. The Steampreneurship through Interdisciplinary Experiential Entrepreneurship curriculum integrates core academic subjects with the principles of entrepreneurship, providing a comprehensive framework that fosters a deep understanding of how to apply entrepreneurial skills in real-world contexts.

Interdisciplinary Approach:
Integration Across Subjects:

English Language Arts (ELA): ELA courses focus on developing communication skills crucial for business, such as writing business plans and pitches, analyzing case studies of business communications, and studying the biographies and writings of successful entrepreneurs. This not only enhances students' language skills but also their understanding of the narratives behind successful business ventures.

Social Studies: The curriculum explores the evolution of economic systems, the impacts of entrepreneurship on society, and global economic dynamics through comparative analyses, case studies, and debates. This helps students grasp the complex socio-economic environments in which businesses operate.

Science: Science education at AA Steam focuses on environmental science and technology, encouraging students to research green technologies and undertake projects that promote sustainable business practices.

Mathematics: Math classes apply concepts to real-world business problems, using statistics for market analysis, budgeting, and financial forecasting. This practical application helps students understand the quantitative aspects of running a business.

Example Modules and Projects:

The Global Product Journey: Students engage in a year-long project that follows a product (e.g., a T-shirt) from conception to sale. This project integrates knowledge from geography, economics, science, and mathematics to give students a comprehensive view of the global supply chain and business operations.

Project-Based Learning:

Real-World Application:
Students are engaged in long-term projects that require them to create mock businesses or develop business plans that address real-world problems. These projects are designed to simulate actual business scenarios, providing students with firsthand experience in entrepreneurship.

Collaboration and Teamwork:
The academy emphasizes teamwork and collaborative learning, reflecting the real-world business environment where cross-disciplinary collaboration is crucial. Students work in interdisciplinary teams, fostering an environment where varied perspectives drive innovation and problem-solving.

Entrepreneurial Guest Speakers and Field Trips:
The curriculum includes interactions with real-world entrepreneurs and visits to local businesses. These activities provide practical insights and inspiration, helping students connect classroom learning with real-world applications.

Assessment:
A blend of traditional tests and innovative assessment methods evaluates students' understanding. This includes project presentations to panels of teachers and external business experts, as well as the compilation and review of portfolios that document students' learning processes and outcomes.

Technology Integration

At AA Steam & Entrepreneurship Academy, technology integration is foundational to delivering the Steampreneurship through Interdisciplinary Experiential Entrepreneurship curriculum effectively. By harnessing modern tools and platforms, the academy will ensure that learning is not only contemporary but also engaging and tailored to meet the demands of today's dynamic business world.

Utilizing Modern Tools:
The academy will employ a range of cutting-edge technologies that significantly enhance the educational experience:

Virtual Reality (VR): VR technology will be utilized to simulate complex business environments and real-world market scenarios, allowing students to experience and navigate the intricacies of various industries without leaving the classroom. This immersive technology helps students understand abstract concepts in a concrete way, preparing them for real-life challenges.

Artificial Intelligence (AI): AI tools will be integrated to provide personalized learning paths for each student. These tools analyze student data to tailor the curriculum, ensuring that each student's learning experience is optimized for their individual pace and style. AI also will aid in identifying students' strengths and areas for improvement, enabling targeted interventions.

Data-Driven Instruction:

AA Steam & Entrepreneurship Academy will embrace a data-driven approach to instruction, which allows for the customization of education to meet the unique needs of each student while ensuring overall academic progress:

Edgenuity Platform: The academy will use Edgenuity, an online learning platform that supports the creation of business-focused content. This platform facilitates instant content assignment and assessment, streamlining the educational process and allowing facilitators to focus more on mentoring rather than administrative tasks.

Analytical Tools: The school will employ advanced data analytics tools to track and analyze student performance continuously. This data is crucial for adapting teaching methods and materials in real-time, ensuring that educational interventions are both timely and effective.

Hybrid Learning Model:
The academy will operate on a hybrid learning model, which combines online and in-person educational experiences:

Macro and Micro Classroom Settings: Each class of 30 students will be divided into three micro-classrooms. This structure allows for more personalized interaction and ensures that each student receives the attention they need to excel. Each micro-classroom is led by one adult facilitator and three student facilitators, promoting leadership among students and enhancing peer learning.

Project Management Groups: Students will work in project management groups, mirroring real-world business environments. These groups foster collaboration and practical problem-solving, with tasks and roles designed to emulate actual business operations.

Promoting a Facilitative Learning Environment:
Role of Facilitators: In this innovative educational setting, teachers will transition from traditional roles to become facilitators of learning. This change emphasizes guiding students through complex projects and helping them apply theoretical knowledge in practical settings.

Student Facilitators: Empowering students to take on facilitative roles encourages leadership and accountability, critical skills in business and entrepreneurship.

Leading Educational Innovation

The integration of technology at AA Steam & Entrepreneurship Academy will exemplify how educational institutions can leverage modern tools to transform learning experiences. This approach not only makes education more relevant to the modern economic landscape but also more compelling and effective for students.

As other schools look to the future, the model implemented at AA Steam & Entrepreneurship Academy serves as a compelling blueprint. It shows that with the right integration of technology, innovative curriculum design, and a focus on experiential learning, schools can not only prepare students for the future but actively shape what that future looks like. This academy is not just teaching students to navigate the world; it is empowering them to change it.

Preparing Future Leaders

AA Steam & Entrepreneurship Academy's Steampreneurship curriculum is a dynamic model designed to equip students with the critical, collaborative, and entrepreneurial skills necessary to navigate and succeed in a globally interconnected economy. The curriculum will prepare students to understand the complexities of global markets and to positively impact those markets.

The academy will be positioned to become a leading example of how educational institutions can effectively combine academic rigor with practical application, preparing students to be the innovative leaders and responsible citizens that the future will require.

Step by Step Steampreneurship Implementation

Step-by-Step Classroom Group Implementation of Steampreneurship at AA STEAM & Entrepreneurship Academy

Macro and Micro Classroom Settings

Each class of 30 students will be divided into three micro-classrooms. This structure allows for personalized interaction and ensures that each student receives the attention they need to excel. Each micro-classroom is led by one adult facilitator and three student facilitators, promoting leadership among students and enhancing peer learning. The classrooms will have daily support from our Instructional Specialist, who will analyze data daily, if not hourly, as part of their role to continuously improve through their own SWOT analysis of classrooms.

Project Management Groups

Students will work in project management groups, mirroring real-world business environments. These groups foster collaboration and practical problem-solving, with tasks and roles designed to emulate actual business operations.

Daily Routine

1. **Project Management App/Google Check and Review (5-10 minutes):**
   - Quick review and setup of project management tools.
2. **Initial SWOT Analysis Setup (30 minutes):**
   - Student Facilitator starts a discussion on the background of the business.
   - Analysts begin researching and documenting the SWOT components using Google Sheets for live collaboration and documentation.
3. **Role-Specific Tasks (30-40 minutes):**
   - Each student works on their assigned role (e.g., Historian, Market Analyst, Product Designer).
4. **Group Collaboration and Integration (20 minutes):**
   - The Project Manager reconvenes the group to integrate findings and prepare for a group presentation.
5. **Edgenuity Station Rotation (30 minutes):**
   - Students rotate through stations focused on GA Standard Exposure and Completion.
6. **Final Review and Daily Presentation Preparation (20 minutes):**
   - Groups prepare their presentation based on the day's work.

7. **Daily Share-Out and Feedback Session (20-30 minutes):**
   - Each group presents their findings and receives feedback from peers and the Adult Facilitator.

Total Session Time: 160-180 minutes

Learning Stations Adaptation

Edgenuity Station: Digital learning tailored to part of the concept being studied.

Entrepreneurship Project Station: Projects tied directly to real-world business case studies.

STEAM Collaborative Learning Station: Applying STEAM skills to solve business problems identified in the SWOT analysis.

Small Group Instruction Station: The adult facilitator rotates through groups to provide targeted guidance.

Engagement and Assessment

Continuous Assessment: Students are assessed on their participation, creativity, and ability to apply interdisciplinary knowledge rather than traditional tests.

Final Project: Students create their own business proposal based on the strengths admired in the Fortune 500 companies analyzed.

Beginning SWOT Group Structure

Student Groups: 8-10 students per group, with a maximum of 30 students per class, divided into three main groups.

Roles Within Each Group:

Student Facilitator: Leads the group, ensuring all voices are heard and tasks are accomplished.

Strengths Analysts (1-2 Students): Identify the strengths of the business case being studied.

Weaknesses Analysts (2 Students): Explore areas of improvement within the business case.

Opportunities Analysts (2 Students): Identify potential growth areas or strategic advantages.

Threats Analysts (1-2 Students): Assess external challenges or risks that the business might face.

Marketing Strategist: Proposes marketing strategies and innovative ways to enhance business visibility.

Problem Solver: Tackles any challenges that arise during the analysis, suggesting feasible solutions.

Adult Facilitator: Supports the group, ensuring resources are available and the group stays on task.

Defined Roles for Student Project Management Team

1. Project Manager: Oversees the entire project, ensures deadlines are met, and coordinates between team members.

2. Historian: Researches the history of the business under study.

3. Market Analyst: Identifies potential markets for the products or services.

4. Product Designer: Designs or reimagines the business's products or services.

5. Supply Chain Coordinator: Examines the supply chain for materials and products, including sustainability practices.

6. Marketing Strategist: Develops marketing campaigns based on SWOT analysis outcomes.

7. Global Strategist: Explores global markets and possibilities for international expansion.

8. Financial Analyst: Manages budget considerations and financial strategies.

9.Technology Officer: Investigates technological solutions for efficiency or product quality improvements.

10. Communications Director: Manages internal and external communications and presentations.

Integration and Workflow

Students convene regularly in project management meetings to discuss their findings and strategies. This approach ensures comprehensive business analysis and teaches the importance of interdisciplinary collaboration and communication.

Culminating Project

The project culminates in a comprehensive presentation where each student presents their findings and contributions, reinforcing the material learned and developing public speaking and presentation skills.

Flexibility and Feedback

Flexibility: The schedule allows for deep discussions or extended tasks as needed.

Feedback Mechanism: Structured feedback is implemented for continuous improvement in presentations and analysis.

Documentation: All work is documented in Google Sheets for accountability and progress tracking.

By gradually releasing responsibility to students, they develop independence and confidence in their abilities to analyze, manage, and present business projects, preparing them for real-world challenges in STEAM and entrepreneurship.

$$\sim\ 11\ \sim$$

REFLECTION AND VISION
FORWARD

As we conclude this exploration of Steampreneurship through Interdisciplinary Experiential Entrepreneurship curriculum at AA Steam & Entrepreneurship Academy, it is imperative to pause and reflect on the broader implications of this pioneering educational model. This journey through the development and planned execution of Steampreneurship highlights a transformative approach to learning—one that prepares students not just to adapt to the future but to actively define it.

Reflective Insights

Educators, policymakers, and all stakeholders in the educational community are invited to consider the impact of the Steampreneurship model. This curriculum does more than educate; it revolutionizes the very fabric of traditional education by embedding the entrepreneurial spirit at its core. It challenges students to think critically, act innovatively, and approach the world as a canvas for their ideas. The potential societal and economic benefits of such an education system are profound. By fostering a generation of solution-oriented thinkers and leaders, we can anticipate a future where challenges are met with creative solutions that are not bound by conventional thinking but are inspired by a deep understanding of interdisciplinary connections.

Implications for Policy and Practice:

Policy Impact: For policymakers, the successful implementation of Steampreneurship at AA Steam & Entrepreneurship Academy serves as a compelling argument for the reform of educational standards and practices at larger scales. It underscores the necessity for curricula that are adaptable, forward-thinking, and aligned with real-world demands.

Educational Practice: Educators are encouraged to adopt and adapt the principles of Steampreneurship, integrating experiential learning and entrepreneurial thinking into their teaching methodologies, irrespective of the subject taught. This adaptation is not just about changing curricula but about transforming educational mindsets to embrace innovation and practicality.

Looking Ahead

The future of education demands continuous innovation and adaptation. As the world evolves, so too must the ways in which we teach and learn. The Steampreneurship model at AA Steam & Entrepreneurship Academy is just the beginning. It is a call to action for educational institutions worldwide to not merely keep pace with global changes but to anticipate and drive them.

Future Directions:

Scalability and Adaptation: The next steps involve scaling the Steampreneurship model to fit different educational contexts and cultures, making it accessible to a broader audience. This scalability will require customization to meet diverse needs, proving that the core principles of Steampreneurship—interdisciplinary learning, experiential focus, and entrepreneurial mindset—are universally applicable.

Continual Improvement: As with any innovative endeavor, the Steampreneurship curriculum will require ongoing refinement and adaptation. This iterative process is vital in ensuring that the education delivered remains relevant, effective, and transformative.

Call to Innovate:

We stand at a pivotal moment in educational history, one in which we have the tools, technology, and insights to fundamentally change how education is delivered and received. Let us seize this opportunity to reimagine the possibilities of education. Let us commit to a future where every learner is empowered to not only face the world's complexities but also construct the solutions that will overcome them.

Conclusion

This book, and particularly the example of AA Steam & Entrepreneurship Academy, serves not only as a guide but also as inspiration. It is proof that when we dare to innovate and apply comprehensive, forward-thinking approaches to education, we prepare our students for more than just careers; we prepare them to be pioneers of their destinies and architects of the world's future. Let this be a call to all who are involved in shaping minds and futures: the time for change is now, and the tools are in our hands. Let us build a legacy of education that truly reflects the capabilities and potential of the next generation.

REFERENCES

1. Piaget, J. (1954). The Construction of Reality in the Child.
2. Vygotsky, L. (1978). Mind in Society: The Development of Higher Psychological Processes.
3. Drucker, P. (1985). Innovation and Entrepreneurship.
4. Kolb, D. A. (1984). Experiential Learning: Experience as the Source of Learning and Development.
5. Ladson-Billings, G. (1995). Toward a Theory of Culturally Relevant Pedagogy. American Educational Research Journal, 32(3), 465-491.
6. National Research Council. (2012). Education for Life and Work: Developing Transferable Knowledge and Skills in the 21st Century.
7. Gates Foundation. (2014). Early Progress on Personalized Learning.
8. Center for Curriculum Redesign. (2015). Four-Dimensional Education: The Competencies Learners Need to Succeed.
9. National Center for Biotechnology Information (NCBI). (2017). Learning Styles: Concepts and Evidence.
10. British Council. (2017). Skills for a global economy: Demand and supply of high-level skills.
11. Manyika, J., et al. (2017). Jobs lost, jobs gained: Workforce transitions in a time of automation. McKinsey Global Institute.
12. OECD (2018). The Future of Education and Skills 2030.
13. Pew Research Center. (2018). Internet/Broadband Fact Sheet.
14. Pew Research Center. (2018). Social Media Use Continues to Rise in Developing Countries but Plateaus Across Developed Ones.
15. Pew Research Center. (2018). Teens, Social Media & Technology 2018.
16. UNESCO (2019). Global Education Monitoring Report: Migration, displacement and education.
17. UNESCO. (2019). Reimagining Our Futures Together: A New Social Contract for Education.

18. World Trade Organization (WTO). (2019). World Trade Statistical Review 2019.

19. American Council on Education (ACE). (2020). Intercultural Competence: What Students Need to Know and Be Able to Do.

20. International Monetary Fund (IMF). (2020). Digital Commerce and Its Impact on the Global Economy.

21. National Center for Education Statistics (NCES). (2020). The Condition of Education 2020.

22. World Economic Forum. (2020). The COVID-19 pandemic has changed education forever. This is how.

23. World Economic Forum (WEF). (2020). The Future of Jobs Report 2020.

24. Organisation for Economic Co-operation and Development (OECD). (2021). Global Competency for an Inclusive World.

25. Ivanov, D. (2020). Predicting the impacts of epidemic outbreaks on global supply chains: A simulation-based analysis on the coronavirus outbreak (COVID-19/SARS-CoV-2) case. Transportation Research Part E: Logistics and Transportation Review, 136, 101922.

26. Villarreal, M. A., & Fergusson, I. F. (2020). The North American Free Trade Agreement (NAFTA) and the United States-Mexico-Canada Agreement (USMCA). Congressional Research Service.

27. Zhou, M., Sari, A. R., & Lee, M. M. (2020). A systematic review of research on open educational resources in the context of accessibility. Educational Technology Research and Development, 68, 1609-1635.

28. Organisation for Economic Co-operation and Development (OECD). (2021). Global Competency for an Inclusive World.

29. O'Dowd, R. (2013). Telecollaboration and online intercultural exchange: A systematic review. Language Teaching, 46(1), 57-80.

30. National Service Learning Clearinghouse. (2020). Impact of Service-Learning on College Students.

31. Association for Psychological Science. (2019). Active Learning Boosts Performance in STEM Courses.

32. National Association of Colleges and Employers (NACE). (2019). Internships and Co-ops.

33. Bell, S. (2010). Project-Based Learning for the 21st Century: Skills for the Future. The Clearing House, 83(2), 39-43.

34. Kuh, G. D. (2008). High-Impact Educational Practices: What They Are, Who Has Access to Them, and Why They Matter. Association of American Colleges and Universities.

35. Siemens, G. (2005). Connectivism: A Learning Theory for the Digital Age.

36. Kolb, A. Y., & Kolb, D. A. (2005). "Learning Styles and Learning Spaces: Enhancing Experiential Learning in Higher Education." Academy of Management Learning & Education, 4(2), 193-212.

37. Liker, J.K., & Choi, T.Y. (2004). Building Deep Supplier Relationships. Harvard Business Review.

38. Jones, C., & English, J. (2004). A contemporary approach to entrepreneurship education. Education + Training, 46(8/9), 416-423.

39. Bellotti, F., Berta, R., De Gloria, A., & Ott, M. (2013). Serious games and the development of an entrepreneurial mindset in higher education engineering students. Entertainment Computing, 4(3), 183-190.

40. Mansilla, V. B., & Jackson, A. (2011). Educating for Global Competence: Preparing Our Youth to Engage the World. Asia Society.

41. Earley, P. C., & Ang, S. (2003). Cultural Intelligence: Individual Interactions Across Cultures. Stanford University Press.

42. Hammer, M. R. (2011). The Intercultural Development Inventory: An Approach for Assessing and Building Intercultural Competence. In M. Moodian (Ed.), Contemporary Leadership and Intercultural Competence.

43. Hunter, B., White, G. P., & Godbey, G. C. (2006). What does it mean to be globally competent? Journal of Studies in International Education, 10(3), 267-285.

44. Ang, S., Van Dyne, L., Koh, C., Ng, K. Y., Templer, K. J., Tay, C., & Chandrasekar, N. A. (2007). Cultural intelligence: Its measurement and effects on cultural judgment and decision making, cultural adaptation and task performance. Management and Organization Review, 3(3), 335-371.

45. Wurdinger, S. D., & Carlson, J. A. (2010). Teaching for experiential learning: Five approaches that work. Rowman & Littlefield Education.

46. Greenhow, C., & Lewin, C. (2016). Social media and education: Reconceptualizing the boundaries of formal and informal learning. Learning, Media and Technology, 41(1), 6-30.

47. Martin, F., & Ertzberger, J. (2016). Here and now mobile learning: An experimental study on the use of mobile technology. Computers & Education, 98, 76-88.

48. Network for Teaching Entrepreneurship. (2019). Entrepreneurship Education and its Impact on Global Economics. NFTE.

49. British Council. (2013). Culture at Work: The value of intercultural skills in the workplace.
50. Freeman, S., Eddy, S. L., McDonough, M., Smith, M. K., Okoroafor, N., Jordt, H., & Wenderoth, M. P. (2014). "Active learning increases student performance in science, engineering, and mathematics." Proceedings of the National Academy of Sciences, 111(23), 8410-8415.
51. Institute for the Future (2017). "Future Work Skills 2020."
52. Bjorklund, E., & Krämer, M. (2019). "Industry-Education Partnerships: A Strategy for Enhancing Education and Workforce Development." Industry and Higher Education, 33(4), 254-262.
53. Saxena, A. (2014). "Non-Governmental Organizations and Their Impact on Education in Developing Countries." Journal of Education and Social Policy, 1(2), 108-114.
54. Wagner, T. (2015). "Creating Innovators: The Making of Young People Who Will Change the World." Scribner.
55. Johnson, L., Adams Becker, S., Estrada, V., & Freeman, A. (2019). "NMC Horizon Report: 2019 Higher Education Edition." The New Media Consortium.
56. Fernandez, C., & Jamet, E. (2021). "The effects of Virtual Reality on Learning Outcomes in Higher Education: A Meta-Analysis." Computers & Education, 173, 104291.
57. Zhou, M., Xu, K., & Zhao, J. (2020). Application of Artificial Intelligence Technology in Distance Education. Journal of Physics: Conference Series, 1549, 042034.

ABOUT THE AUTHOR

Dr. Anton Anthony, Ed. S, ThD founder and creator of AA Steam & Entrepreneurship and the trademark pedagogy Steampreneurship has served in school districts throughout Georgia as a teacher, discipline coordinator, coach, assistant principal, principal, and district human resource professional.

He has worked in poverty-stricken schools where most of the population was Title I. He has also worked in schools where parents were highly educated, high-income professionals and business owners. Each school brought its own challenges, but he was able to break through barriers and achieve academic improvement everywhere he went.

Credentials

Dr. Anthony received his Bachelor of Arts with Honors in Business Management from Fort Valley State University in Georgia. He received his Masters of Arts in Teaching at Augusta State University. He later returned to receive a degree in Curriculum and Instruction from Augusta University and received his Educational Specialist add-on in Educational Leadership and Administration, also at Augusta University. His Doctorate in Theology was awarded from North Central Theological Seminary. He is a licensed educator and real estate broker with the State of Georgia.

Career

He began his educational career as a reading specialist in Burke County, Georgia schools. He was moved into the 7th grade English/Language Arts program (ELA), where he experienced his first real taste of educational success. His class achieved the highest passing percentage, and he was given an award to recognize his achievement.

After spending a second year at the middle school where he began his career, he asked for a position as a coach at an alternative school in that same district. Former teacher of the year for the school, he was allowed to become the coach, discipline coordinator, and reading instructor. From those positions, he would become an assistant principal and principal.

Current Status

Mr. Anthony currently lives in Georgia. He is a resource professional for the 3rd largest school district in Georgia and looks forward to bringing his vision of AA STEAM & Entrepreneurship Academy to life.

CONTACT THE AUTHOR

Contact Information
To connect with Mr. Anthony online, you can find him online.

Website
lovingeducation.org

Facebook: http://facebook.com/anton.anthony1
Twitter:
https://Twitter.com/antonanthony5

Instagram:
Instagram.com/oracle_of_education

LinkedIn:
www.linkedin.com/in/authorantonanthonysr

YouTube:
https://www.youtube.com/channel/UCI77nqy8OXItxQ_ZazNSm0w

Email:
antonanthonysr@gmail.com

contact@lovingeducation.org

AAStemAcademy@gmail.com

www.ingramcontent.com/pod-product-compliance
Lightning Source LLC
Chambersburg PA
CBHW060906140726
47996CB00001B/138